Deconstructed Do-Gooder

MISSIONAL WISDOM LIBRARY
RESOURCES FOR CHRISTIAN COMMUNITY

The Missional Wisdom Foundation experiments with and teaches about alternative forms of Christian community. The definition of what constitutes a Christian community is shifting as many seek spiritual growth outside of the traditional confines of church. Christians are experimenting with forming communities around gardens, recreational activities, coworking spaces, and hundreds of other focal points, connecting with their neighbors while being aware of the presence of God in their midst. The Missional Wisdom Library series includes resources that address these kinds of communities and their cultural, theological, and organizational implications.

Series Editor: Larry Duggins

Deconstructed Do-Gooder

A Memoir About Learning Mercy the Hard Way

Britney Winn Lee

FOREWORD BY
D. L. Mayfield

CASCADE *Books* • Eugene, Oregon

DECONSTRUCTED DO-GOODER
A Memoir About Learning Mercy the Hard Way

Missional Wisdom Library: Resources for Christian Community 7

Cascade Books
An Imprint of Wipf and Stock Publishers
199 W. 8th Ave., Suite 3
Eugene, OR 97401

www.wipfandstock.com

PAPERBACK ISBN: 978-1-5326-3121-4
HARDCOVER ISBN: 978-1-5326-3123-8
EBOOK ISBN: 978-1-5326-3122-1

Cataloguing-in-Publication data:

Names: Lee, Britney Winn, author. | Mayfield, D. L., foreword.

Title: Deconstructed do-gooder : a memoir about learning mercy the hard way / by Britney Winn Lee ; foreword by D.L. Mayfield.

Description: Eugene, OR: Cascade Books, 2019 | Missional Wisdom Library: Resources for Christian Community Series 7 | Includes bibliographical references.

Identifiers: ISBN 978-1-5326-3121-4 (paperback) | ISBN 978-1-5326-3123-8 (hardcover) | ISBN 978-1-5326-3122-1 (ebook)

Subjects: LCSH: Christian life. | Christian biography—United States | Church and the world.

Classification: BV4526.3 L465 2019 (print) | BV4526.3 (ebook)

Manufactured in the U.S.A.   04/15/19

For Bridger, whose birth woke me up and made me tender to a world that God so loves.

I hope your road is mercy-filled.

There was a scholar of the law who stood up to test him and said, "Teacher, what must I do to inherit eternal life?" Jesus said to him, "What is written in the law? How do you read it?" He said in reply, "You shall love the Lord, your God, with all your heart, with all your being, with all your strength, and with all your mind, and your neighbor as yourself." He replied to him, "You have answered correctly; do this and you will live." But because he wished to justify himself, he said to Jesus, "And who is my neighbor?" Jesus replied, "A man fell victim to robbers as he went down from Jerusalem to Jericho. They stripped and beat him and went off leaving him half-dead. A priest happened to be going down that road, but when he saw him, he passed by on the opposite side. Likewise a Levite came to the place, and when he saw him, he passed by on the opposite side. But a Samaritan traveler who came upon him was moved with compassion at the sight. He approached the victim, poured oil and wine over his wounds and bandaged them. Then he lifted him up on his own animal, took him to an inn and cared for him. The next day he took out two silver coins and gave them to the innkeeper with the instruction, 'Take care of him. If you spend more than what I have given you, I shall repay you on my way back.' Which of these three, in your opinion, was neighbor to the robbers' victim?" He answered, "The one who treated him with mercy." Jesus said to him, "Go and do likewise."

Contents

Foreword

"You either die a hero, or live long enough to see yourself become the villain."—Harvey Dent

THERE ARE SOME PEOPLE, who, for whatever reason, are born to be deeply religious souls. When done right, excavating the inner workings of these kinds of people is interesting, profound, and deeply unsettling. To read of young children who so badly want to follow God and do everything right—and feel a moral obligation to then share what they have learned—is to watch one of the most longstanding operas unfold. It's the story of the soul who thought they got everything right about God, until the world convinced them otherwise.

What happens next in these kinds of stories is always intriguing to me. Does the person become more doggedly determined to figure things out? Do they escape into the easiness of tradition and orthodoxy, allowing those long dead and distinguished to make the arguments for them? Do they become fundamentalists, unable to see the gray in the cracks of the world, never for a moment allowing themselves to believe they could be wrong? Or do they slowly let it slip away, never to trouble their minds again, easing into a life of ambiguities and unknowns?

In Britney Winn Lee's hands, this kind of story becomes something else altogether: a series of revelations, reimagingings, failings, and ultimately, kindness toward oneself and others. It is a combination of all the ways religious folks have struggled with their own complicated desires to be good, and to prove it to God and to others.

Her story, set through the lens of each and every character in the parable of the Good Samaritan, is itself an invitation to those who have struggled with religiosity. I couldn't help but think of the Ignatian spiritual practice of Lectio Divina as I read this book—about how powerful the Bible can be when we allow ourselves to imagine different possibilities and fresh kinds of revelation. Like Lee, I grew up very devout—the daughter of evangelical pastors, homeschooled, on track to be a missionary to the lost and the lonely. I grew up understanding that you read the Bible, understood the plain and clear meaning, and went out to tell everyone what you knew.

How hard it is to let go of these hierarchies we were born into, or that we created for ourselves! Learning to approach the Bible with wide eyes and open hands has been a hard lesson to learn. I would prefer sometimes to be done with the Scriptures, and all the verses I had cherry-picked that made me feel good and comfortable and safe. But here, in this book, Lee offers another way. She invites us to set aside our own agendas, to practice a little of your own Lectio Divina. Where are you surprised to find yourself in the story, both now and in the past?

This deep-dive into the Good Samaritan parable brought to mind Dr. Martin Luther King Jr., who tried to live his life in the light of what it means to love his neighbor—even the one who wants to harm him. King identifies another character in this parable, a character found throughout the pages of this memoir: the country that creates the situations leading up to the Jericho road being so unsafe. As he said, "One day we must come to see that the whole Jericho road must be transformed so that men and women will not be constantly beaten and robbed as they make their journey on life's highway. True compassion is more than flinging a coin to a beggar; it is not haphazard and superficial. It comes to see that an edifice which produces beggars needs restructuring."

Lee practices the work of mercy and compassion on herself in this book—and gives us the gift of that insight. She is and remains someone who wants to be the hero of the story—even as she contains the ambivalent, the cruel, the misguided, the longing-to-be-justified parts as well. Her story is important, because it rests on this understanding of true compassion of MLK: are we ready to see everything made new? Including our histories and structures and societies and policies that have hinged on creating both the robbers and the robbed?

There was room for me in this book; I suspect there is room for you too. With humor, insight, and self-reflection, Lee invites us to consider all the ways we are a part of the story playing out around us. And in the end, it is our brokenness that will save us, because our brokenness binds us to one another in ways that are based on mutuality and equity. We are never only the robber, we are never only the wounded, we are never only the good Samaritan. We are people, in our own small ways, who long to be good, even as we fail in somewhat spectacular ways to reach this goal.

This is a memoir of new monasticism, a work of narrative theology, a story of continual deconstruction and reconstruction. And in the end, it invites the reader to think about their own roles in this, the most famous story of Jesus. The hero, the villain—or something in between? May you read it, be encouraged, and consider what it might mean to work towards entire systems that are built to take care of our most vulnerable.

D.L. Mayfield, author of *Assimilate or Go Home: Notes from a Failed Missionary on Rediscovering Faith*

Acknowledgements

NEVER AGAIN WILL I downplay the importance of a book's acknowledgement section. Whereas I once saw all of the bindings displayed on our 1970s dining room bookshelves as representing single-person works, now I cannot un-see the undoubtable villages that are associated with each. No one writes a book alone. I've relied deeply and gratefully on so many during these last two years.

To the crew at Cascade Books, thank you for taking a chance on my voice; it has helped me to further find and form it. To Jonathan, who didn't have to be as accessible and generous of a presence as you have been since Collegeville: thank you. Danielle, your writing was some of the first to teach me about the beauty and connection that can be found in sharing tension and ending a prose unresolved. I feel so honored that you would spend your hours crafting this book's foreword.

To my first-read team who helped me to rip the Band-Aid off of what I was really trying to say: you gifted me with the breakthrough I needed. Joel, Jennifer, June, Callie, Chris, Erin, Anna: your feedback told me to keep going and to put a flag in the word *mercy* as vitally important. Thank you for loving me enough to embrace this book's (as Anne Lamott would say) "shitty first draft" with gentleness and care. A thousand apologies for the grammatical jungle through which I asked you to wade (during the holidays, no less). Erin, thank you for your canyon of insight and for being another female voice on this New Monastic/writer road who stood ahead with a lantern and a waving arm. Your company is rich.

I have so much gratitude for Jennifer, who reminded me at the very beginning to not forget the praying. I have heard your voice at every block and in every vulnerable meltdown.

To my parents, Connie and Benjie, who have always pushed their walls open wider for the fatherless, the widow, and the way-finding young adult: I cannot reach deeply enough to find the "thank you" that does justice to how I feel. You have defined generosity and home for me long before I even realized their eternal and universal importance. And I have never not felt as if you were wholeheartedly in my corner (despite the anxiety that my antics and risks have caused you). Thank you for making fertile soil that could hold the seeds of an evolving faith.

To you both and to my wonderfully supportive in-laws (Patty and Donny), thank you for all of the afternoons, nights, and weekends that you offered to play with our boy so that I could hammer out another essay. You have been excited for and so helpful to us when you truly could have been little more than worried about our transitions and processes. Thank you for the space and help in becoming who we are becoming as individuals and as a family.

To my college chapel community, former roommates, fellow Haiti travelers, and Yellow House family: you taught me more about God and about myself than I ever could have dreamed would be possible in ten short years. I have glimpsed full life because of your companionship and your will to get close, be honest, choose love, and stick around. Wherever you are and go, you take a sacred piece of me with you.

Thank you, Highland, for letting me grow up on your blocks. Thank you "John" and so many other forgiving and merciful souls who keep showing me the love of Jesus. Thank you to the friends that I have made in the melding fires of motherhood and those who have stuck with me through every character I have been thus far; who hold up my arms and my spirit on the days when I give us all whiplash from quickly shifting emotions. I would go insane without you. *Insane.*

Bridger Oaks—my very brave, funny, and sensitive son—will you ever know what you unlocked inside of me? Thank you for existing, for bearing God's image, for giving me one more critical reason to work towards a better world. I should also thank your teacher, Ms. June, who has kept you learning, entertained, and fed on Fridays so that I could write.

Luke, you have given me so much room to grieve and grow. Throughout the changes of these years, I am so thankful to know that home is with you, no matter what and no matter where. Thank you for seeing me as a writer before I would ever allow myself to say it. I love you deeply and choose you daily, forever and ever.

And to anyone who bought or borrowed this book, sincerely thank you. You get one wild, beautiful, important life, and I don't take it lightly that you would spend some of it reading a little bit about mine. I'm so grateful to God for getting to be in this world, for the chances to discover and rediscover the mysteries of faith, and to have lived long enough to experience sweet mercy and the incredible joy and healing that has come with writing about it.

Introduction

THIS BOOK IS ABOUT seeking religious faithfulness, experiencing unavoidable need, and encountering unexpected mercy. It is a story about wanting to be right and good and assuming that one can hold all the answers to the questions of how we should be walking on a road that follows Jesus. It's a book that explores the journey of one self-proclaimed way-knower (hi) as she migrates over the course of fifteen years through each character in the story of the Good Samaritan. It is series of theological narratives about reconstructing my role in the life of faith again and again before my disappointments and deconstructions could swallow me whole.

It's about all that we do to not be wrong or in need when it comes to God; and it's about learning (the hard way) how that is maybe missing the point. I think that you'll find it to be an important account—though it is only mine—as our current times, especially within Christianity, can seem so unmerciful.

So you and I are going to time-travel a bit. And listen, I'm a sucker for time-travel. When I first watched *Back to the Future*, belatedly as an adult, I grew so giddy seeing Christopher Lloyd yell "Eighty-eight miles per hour!" while the license plate spun unrealistically amidst the flames racing under Michael J. Fox's feet. I immediately googled "Back to the Future King Size bed sheets" to solidify my fandom like a ten-year-old. Except, I was twenty-six, and married, and pregnant.

The thought of time travel is so novel, full-circle, quirky, sometimes tragic, often thematic regarding messages of dark, and light, and well-used moments. *What I know now that I didn't know then. What I did then that made all the difference now.* Memoir writing is a lot like time travel. I'm honored, albeit a good bit nervous, to be returning to these versions of myself with you.

We'll start my story where the Scripture's story begins: at the seeker (or the lawmaker) whose question drives the whole parable. *"Teacher, what must I do . . ."* Having been raised in an evangelical, Bible-Belt environment, my seeker-drive quickly absorbed the rule-abiding religiosity of the priest in the narrative who most likely honored rules and undoubted answers, until she no longer could. College, and all of its diversity, would go on to offer convincing rationale for me to step into the less regulated role of the Levite who still prioritized purity (possibly over people), but who was maybe a bit more approachable than the priest since historically and culturally she would have been held to less rigid standards.

Young adulthood and a breath-stealing baptism into the reality of poverty and inequality would throw my world into that of the Samaritan (at least how I defined her at the time). And I'd live in the land of outreach and missions until I realized how impossible it was to exist there without the stability of the innkeeper. New-Monasticism and Emergent Christianity would bring a concept of anchored, shared living to compassion work; and I would think that I'd finally arrived at the utmost potential for my faith within the company of a beloved community who could help shoulder the repercussions of the world's nastiest robbers (who were, to me, disconnected evangelicals).

But then, my idealism began to break down once again, this time faster than I could repair it.

But then, we buried an orphan's casket, and faced unavoidable loss to cancer, and chose our safety over marching on behalf of the marginalized.

But then, a series of events took place that made me question whether I was the story's rescuer or the ruinous and exploitative thief.

But then, people we had made promises to and with moved.

But then, our son was born.

And we closed the doors on everything we'd spent ten years working toward.

But then, the downward spiral of depression, anxiety, and identity crisis took over everything.

But then, I was left in pieces on a roadside, waiting and hoping to die, when I'd only ever wanted to do good and walk well.

But then, I had made my way through every character of the tale, desperately attempting to figure out how Jesus wanted me (and therefore, everyone) to live, until there was no one else left to be.

I gather that most folks expect one faith deconstruction in their lives. I, unprepared for multiple deconstructions, found myself in the last years of my twenties spinning like a mouse in a self-concocted maze, over-correcting at every wrong turn, and speeding off to the next ideal before I could realize that I might be lost; I might know less; I might feel pain. I spun until there were no more turns to make—just bleakness and exhaustion.

It takes a lot of time and energy to uphold the walls that you think may kill you.

But then mine fell.

And I woke up.

Always testing his divinity and wit, one of the experts of the law asked Jesus how he might acquire real life forever and ever. Jesus pointed him back to the old words of the Jewish tradition instructing us to love God with our whole being and to love our neighbors as we love ourselves. Then Jesus, telling his riddle-like story of the beaten man and his line-up of commuters, asks, "Which of these three do you think was a neighbor?" The lawman, apparently answering correctly, identifies that it was indeed the one full of mercy.

"Go and do likewise," Jesus responds. Go and do likewise, we are encouraged.

Go, love God and love your neighbor who is the one full of mercy, the Samaritan, the one who is both exposing and connecting to your humanity as he reaches out a hand. Love that one as you love yourself.

. . . As you love yourself: you, on the ground; you, who are in need; you, who now know your need.

Over thirty years of hearing, and sharing, and comparing my life to the same old story, and I never knew that I was the wounded one until I was the wounded one.

After all this time, after all these efforts that I will share with you now, I better understand resurrection because I better understand death. As I chased that moving target of faithful living throughout youth and young adulthood, I learned that being a Jesus-follower in God's big world meant more than the ever-convoluted answers I was refining or the ever-changing movements I was championing. It meant dying and then living. It meant knowing and then forgiving. It meant tension and mystery. It meant holding most things but love loosely. It meant living with and connecting to complex and wounded people as a complex and wounded person within the old wineskin systems that are hard on the holding. It meant maybe letting those skins burst in order for something entirely new to form—something like mercy.

It meant, truly, losing my way to find it.

This is a memoir about chasing, deconstructing, and reimagining the theology of my teens and twenties. But it is also a story about a complicated faith journey that went from believing, to doing, to what I think may be becoming. I found light on the other side of an ideological ending (or six) that illuminated what mercy may mean.

I found more light, less fear, and increased hope in a love that connects us all and that cannot fail.

My prayer is that, in whatever character you find yourself while reading (if you do), more light, less fear, and an increased hope is what you leave with as well.

So, with that, a couple of notes before we begin . . .

This is a theological memoir, and my theology has been shaped most and most consistently by God through people. Every story shared represents an era that was drenched in quality friendships, familial relationships, and encounters with strangers and neighbors in which I do not dive extensively enough to do them justice for what they have meant to my soul. I want you to know that for every name you read, there are eight others not mentioned who have been the richest parts of my life and faith, by far. What you're getting are simply the book-tabs for a series of conversions that were guided and nurtured by a village, always. Secondly, the few names that you will read have been mostly changed, since what I share is my perception of our experiences, and their versions are theirs to tell.

And lastly, I wrote each section as if I were functioning out of whatever understanding of God and God's world that I had at the time. The arc of this memoir is leading toward the realization that we are all journeying and that none of us are limited to how we experience each other in any given moment. So I ask for your love and patience as you read through each version. This woman is becoming someone like we are all becoming someone.

Now. Shall we?

Tell Me The Way

The Seeker

The sun-beaten clothes on the line behind him are as blank as some of the faces in the crowd. They are hoping your questions are traps for this self-proclaimed guru to make him pay for the delusional ideas he's been spewing. You are secretly hoping that you're right, that he's right. That whatever chasm of questions your soul has been carving might be bridged here by his words.

But some of the flock's attention is raptured by the teacher's patience and passion. As the little village leans in, you find that you're allowing yourself to lean in as well. Good people trust him, and you very much want to be good.

"Tell me the way," you whisper.

Tell me the way . . .

"What's most important?" your voice cracks. You're desperate.

"What do you already know?" he prompts.

"What God has told us." Your face blotches as you grow more nervous. Oh, how you hate that it does that.

"That's right," he nods.

Thank God . . .

"But wait! But wait. Wait, please, can you clarify? Be specific. Spell it out exactly how we are to do what we are to do." Your words feel a bit indignant now rushing past your tongue as you realize how gone this moment will soon be and how lost you still feel.

His response, a story about who does and doesn't stop for the wounded, seems right enough though you hardly understand it. But maybe it was not to be understood as much as it was to be known and repeated in case someone else were to ask. You and the crowd wanted answers, and he has given them.

It was good to know answers and to hold company with answer-knowers, you conclude.

What Does Jesus Eat?

LET'S TAKE A TRIP. Grab the remote control for the DeLorean. The year is 1997.

Darlene Zchech's "Shout to the Lord" is being recreated in a local sanctuary on a slick black piano made for concertos and cantatas. For all the ways that we did not measure up to Hillsong, there is power pumping among my congregation of mostly older, mostly middle-class, mostly white, country Methodists as we reach the words "praise to our King!" I'm only nine at the time, but even I can feel it.

My WWJD bracelets are stacked on my wrist with the black and neon green one at the bottom because of how it makes me feel most like me. They descend in relatability down my arm and convey a spirituality that is directly proportionate to their number so that the unbelievers might never question my loyalty to the Lord. Back home, the hotline number for the 700 Club is written on a piece of paper in my desk drawer. I call it sometimes for prayer when I need help with my unbelief. I have on a skirt, but its length appropriateness would have been checked with the width of a dollar bill. Ensured that the space between the bottom hem and the top of my knee wasn't greater than George Washington's face, I could leave the house. I am repeating the Apostle's Creed but thinking about all the T-shirts that are being sold at the Lifeway an hour away, how they turn "worldly" logos into Christian messages. I consider them as if they are the next Billy Graham movement. "If only we could have spiritual relevance like that!" I'd be thinking.

Too scared to attend the upcoming Heaven and Hell production because of how similar they were to haunted houses, I'm likely planning to compensate my faithfulness by starting a club among my cousins called Krist's Kids where we spend our time painting wooden signs with Scripture and talking about how we'll be kind for Jesus. We'll pray for our family members while out by the barn gate and discuss tactics one might use to convince passersby to pull over and take part in revival—much like a lemonade stand, but holier.

This is the context of one Jesus-following, do-gooder's beginning:

True Love Waits. Left Behind. Tiny pencils to draw on tiny offering envelopes during worship. Fried chicken at the potluck amidst all the deviled eggs and strawberry sheet cake. Canned food drives. The songs "Butterfly Kisses" and "Days of Elijah." Communion cups holding just enough Welch's Grape Juice to make you want more. Memorizing John 3:16 and pledges to the Christian Flag, the Bible, and America. Watching *Sister Act* and wishing our church could have a "Just a Touch of Love" moment even just one time. Playing an Australian tour guide in the Vacation Bible School skit. Joining the middle-aged women in the hand bell choir because Sandy had "gotten too busy" to "keep up with her commitments to God." Never being able to find the seat-belts in the church van. Praying the Believer's Prayer (to be safe) any chance it was offered over, and over, and over again.

Belief was a predominant theme for spirituality during my upbringing, so much so that one raised in a similar context could plausibly read that statement and feel confused about what could be meant by faith if not belief. This theme was in full force during my childhood as many evangelical communities like mine worked tirelessly to preserve and invest in the pillars of Believer's

Baptism and the Believer's Decision. Worship songs declared it; revivals reproduced it. What we knew and what we claimed were of utmost importance, lest the world were to get its hands on us—we'd seen it happen.

Apologetics courses were prioritized so that those following Christ could give an account when asked about Islam, or homosexuality, or why it was necessary for God's own son to be executed. Invitation times were carved into every sermon, rally, wedding, and funeral to give unbelievers and believers alike a chance to make things right. Words were repeated, cards were signed, and congregations let out yelps of celebration at the listed names of those saved from hell and the return of backsliders who had been having a little too much fun for a little too long.

Responses to life's big questions might vary some, but they were necessary to have and to have ready all the same.

The supply of answers that I built and maintained said that unmarried sex was bad, as were drugs, as would be being gay if it wasn't so foreign. Islam and Buddhism were wrong. Alcohol, cussing, and divorce were common, but things for which we would ask forgiveness (often by way of aisle-walking at revivals). Scripture was factual and infallible. Sundays were sacred. And God's blessings equated to our obedience by way of church attendance, boldness in prayer, memorization of Scripture, and the discipline to reign in our bodies, our mouths, and our doubts. Even less about practicing these values, faith seemed to pertain to knowing them. *We may not do right, but we know right, which means we could one day do right if we could ever get ourselves to get right.* Most importantly, we were able to instruct the others.

This was the religion that built my religion, that first constructed my walls of self-expectation and spirituality. In my embryonic search for faithfulness, I'd deduced that to know what was right was to live righteously by caring about our neighbors enough to help them know what was right as well. I would depend for years on my ability to read what did and did not merit the praise of right-knowing adults in order to map my path of loving

God and loving neighbor like I loved myself—namely, to not let either of us end up in hell.

So this is where we start, in the realm of belief-centric, 1990s evangelical, Southern Christianity. We start in 1997, when God loved mimes in worship and the sun loved lemon juice in hair (only never quite enough to turn a brunette all the way platinum).

I remember my brown hair turning orange in the summers during those months that I'd spend as a child bobbing around our above-ground pool, mulling over ideas about how one might live the most meaningful life. From an early age, I felt certain that there was a great purpose for which to live, recognizing on some elementary level that we get this one shot at existing. I didn't want to waste it on being anything less than a dreamer (or anything darker than a blonde).

As a small-town Louisiana girl raised on country land named after her great-great-granddaddy, if I wasn't occupied by bossing my cousins into thematic adventures around the ponds, or barns, or roadside revivals, I could be found alone and introspective— *thinking too hard*, as my dad would say. The day I figured out how I would live a life worthy of being called *life*, I was alone in our backyard pool surrounded by smells of too much chlorine and cooked, citrusy hair.

While dodging floating, flying-ant clusters, I rifled through the mental Rolodex of causes to be considered. There was the feeding of hungry children, adopting mangled dogs from Sarah McLachlan, or halting the spread of drugs and forest fires (all of the efforts I'd been exposed to at that point by way of commercials and Special Offering Sundays). There certainly was the option of saving whales, which people on my parents' nighttime news seemed to think important enough for sign-making and yelling. I did love *Free Willy* a lot, so I figured this wouldn't be too terribly difficult to get behind.

But with each consideration, I felt limited. As valiant as these plights were, I believed within me that they were not enough; that they did not, even all combined, seem to encompass the level of purpose I needed to account for a life-well-lived.

"What must I do . . .?" I felt the very question that the seeker asked of Jesus growing insatiably within my ribs.

After much mind-racking, an idea came to me as fingers pruned and the sun settled lower into the evening's earth. *If God was Creator, and all of the worthy causes in the world fell inside of creation, then faith would give me the most options to do the most good. To be the most good; to confidently pack my years with well-stewarded minutes; to not have any regrets when they'd all been used up.*

I would live my life for God. It was decided.

One Sunday morning following, I tugged the Astrovan keys out of my mom's hands in an effort to move the family train along once it had stalled at the Mrs. Peggy's and Mrs. Jeans's of the after-church crowd. The most drawn-out fellowship happened in those twelve to twelve-thirty minutes on the sizzling church stairs, bulletins in hand. This particular day, I seemed to be the only one remembering our unlikelihood of beating the Baptists to Chick-a-Dilly if we did not get to getting.

Crouched on the floor of our second row seats, beckoning my parents with glaring eyeballs and the occasional honk, I thought about the lesson my Aunt Kathryn had shared earlier that morning in Sunday school: things about coming to Jesus and making a decision in your heart. It seemed uncomfortable and, though I didn't have words for it, quite abstract. But it also sounded like what good people did, what God-people did eventually. And I was in fact a good God-person now, so why not embrace the inevitable?

There, as cars of more fortunate kids with less talkative families pulled out from behind and in front, I folded into the itchy layer of my appropriately long skirt, and I asked God if I could follow his son Jesus. Then I waited. I pictured Jesus teleporting into the organ that is my heart. I wondered what he'd eat once he got there, thinking how odd it was for someone so big to be made so small.

There was no body-consuming adrenaline, no loud voice, and no tears; not even a ton of assurance that I'd done it correctly or had the wherewithal to write down the exact date and time of salvation like some of my friends had been accustomed to doing. There were just a few insecure words uttered like a spell into a van that would soon hold a solid Sunday fight with my little brother and a box of Chick-a-Dilly's finest.

I had been saved, I thought. I hoped. Because I'd said with my mouth and also maybe with my spirit that God was real, and that I believed it. Belief was so important, if not most important, I was learning from our little corner of the world. Belief in God, belief in his Son, and belief in the words they'd collaborated on together in Scripture. If I began my faith journey as the expert in the law—as the seeker who prompted Jesus with the question *what must I do*—then I first understood his answer as such: loving the Lord my God meant believing him, and loving my neighbor as myself meant making sure that others did as well.

On the car ride back, my grandfather pressed us for what we liked about the things the preacher-man had said that morning. Figuring we were being tested (and I couldn't be seen as a failure, what with Jesus now having *something* for supper in my chest), I recounted words that the pastor had spoken back at the pulpit, surprising us all.

"Hot damn, if that baby wasn't actually listening!" my pappaw beamed, his reaction letting me know that it would be important to pay attention from that point on. Good girls listen to sermons. God-girls who were living their most meaningful lives could get something out of sermons.

But as the weeks trudged on, Sundays for the most part would prove to be little more than a chore. Everything about them felt and smelled old. I was willing to play the game, and please the people, and do what needed to be done; but it was work to value those predictably energy-lacking songs and the number of minutes we were expected to remain fidgetless. I wondered if adulthood would bring with it some sort of genuine appreciation, some sort of epiphany as to why it really mattered that we were talking and singing about what we were talking and singing about.

This much seemed to be true for those present: the goal of belief was not so much about enjoyment as it was about obedience, and right-knowing, and holding onto both when times got tough. And they would.

Declared Resolved

"I'm closing my eyes! You tell me when to turn right and left!" she yelled from the front of the four-wheeler.

"I don't want to do this! Let me off!" I hollered back, terrified. It hadn't been a whole year since I'd signed her cast from the last time she'd done this with a friend. She was so proud of the hole left in the side of her house. I was so regretful about having not grabbed a helmet.

"You're no fun!" she threw out, slamming me into the hole where little women worry so early on about being liked. I wanted to be fun almost as much as I wanted to be good. More than both, I wanted to live long enough to have the meaningful life upon which God and I had agreed a few years before. *I'm going to be so mad at her if she takes that from me*, I brooded, tightening my legs like a clamp behind hers.

"Right. Left. LEFT LACY, GOD!" I shrieked, quickly praying to be spared from early death-by-pine-trees so long as I never used God's name in vain like that again.

She chuckled as we dismounted, heading inside for slumber party activities containing fewer risks for eleven-year-olds. I glanced to the clouds and whispered, "pinky promise," while trying to snap out of the anger that my fear so often produced.

We were wrapping up the less dangerous half of the morning with a craft activity when the final grains of our not-quite-completed sand art bottles ran out. The moment felt tragic and tense as if our agreeable day (that I had salvaged by succumbing to "being fun") might spiral into a snippy fight at any second. But then, fortunately for our friendship and my sanity (two things that often were at odds), I remembered all was not lost.

"We are Christians!" I declared, "We have help!"

Dragging Lacy out to the unsodded patch of yard beside her carport stairs, we scooped dark dirt into swively, swoopy bottles. We prayed that God would change their tints and texture into vibrant, smooth sand. I pressed my eyes shut, like she'd done earlier in the day, and imagined the bright sherbet, fuchsia, and aqua that would be in our near future. I felt nervous and also thrilled that it may turn out that I was indeed the one brave enough to first lead her into a version of her faith where mountains moved and tints turned.

"We need this, Lord. Save us from being sad, from arguing, from not having what we want. What would granting this harm, God?" I could not imagine one reason in the universe for the Lord to withhold this from two people who loved him.

The prayer kept going—as they can when one's worried about the answer.

"In Jesus's name," we remembered to add, sealing the deal just as we'd been taught.

Then, reluctantly peeking through, I was overcome with hurt and embarrassment.

There, in all of their moist normalcy, were jars and jars of regular, disappointing dirt that God couldn't be bothered with touching.

I go back to this moment whenever I am tempted to think that children are too young for existential dread or theological upheaval. It was so sophomoric, and yet, it was the first time that I remember feeling like God wasn't all that much near; the first time I wondered if I understood anything about this God; the first time I felt compelled to swiftly justify and defend God's negligent behavior.

"I guess we didn't have enough faith. We should both probably work on that," I quickly concluded before doubts could either be confirmed or of influence. "We don't understand, but we don't have to," I'd heard the older people say.

Faith meant to trust regardless, so trust regardless we would. And suspicion would be stifled as it had to be. Utter belief was what I'd understood to be the mark of faithfulness. It's what I had gleaned from memorizing words in sermons that were written to answer the seeker's question. And on the day that Jesus returned to gather us up, I would not be "found sleeping," tossed to and fro by the waves of unmet sand expectations. So, I declared myself resolved.

But when my parents retrieved me, I left masking the distance that had been introduced to my spirit that afternoon.

What was God about and for if not our actual lives? What did it mean to have and know the answers, if they didn't seem to matter? If belief didn't provide for or protect us, what was the point in believing? I shoved these thoughts back down into the part of my soul that needed to be reprimanded, deciding to deal with them instead in moments that were less easy to overlook.

Storms Bring the Flowers

Typically, the hallway under the stairs was used for quick escapes out of the office during hide and seek. My grandparents' farm home—consisting of eleven rooms and a wrap-around porch just down the road from our house—was built in the 1920s and had withstood five generations of bad weather. Its bones were strong, creak and groan as they might.

I'd unfolded myself out from under a twin-sized mattress that we'd stuffed into that hallway along with bottled water, books, dolls, and a wheel-crank radio. Noting how versatile the mattress was (with it having just been used as a staircase-roller-coaster car hours before) I joined the adults on the porch. Adults seemed to want to watch the storms. Maybe they were more enthralled and less threatened by their roar. Maybe they were determined to look in the face what they couldn't control.

They sat in the wicker chairs lining the red brick columns. I watched the sooty clouds roll in over the surrounding pastures peppered by clusters of Angus cattle who huddled together in an attempt to coach their anxiety back into submission, as I was trying to do with mine. I depended on the grownups' knowledge, trusting they would know exactly what we were looking for and when it would be sending us back into the bunker that was the windowless hallway where we couldn't be touched.

With ancient-looking kerosene lamps and large bus-yellow flashlights scattered about, we'd wait it out together. I would wonder what made us so different from those houses and lives plowed over in Oklahoma.

The night when one of the bigger ones came through and blustered down our road like it was on the evening stroll of an elderly power-walker, we crouched tightly like a well-played game of Tetris (except one that smelled of fried deer meat and wet, Deep South air). Someone would make a joke, someone would get angry and short, defenses colliding. I paid attention to my breathing and how it quickened the more I tried to pace it.

Being fascinated with World War II novels throughout all of junior high, I cringed at the idea of my family ever being required to be still for as long as Jewish families had been. We were the Portokalos (from the movie *My Big Fat Greek Wedding*) of North Louisiana. Being stuffed into a closet and told, no matter what, not to make a peep would have been our demise, I knew it. *But, I'd suppose, I guess you can do anything if you're scared enough.*

As the funnel passed, shaking its body like a hula hooper, I prayed and cried and felt so out of control. "The storm brings the thunder. The thunder brings the rain. The rain makes the flowers grow," I'd recite just as my mom had taught me to do through heavy winds. Within minutes, all would be safe, and stable, and dull again.

"Thank the Lord," we'd say, only slightly disappointed that the energizing drama had subsided.

Why did God make storms that kill and scare people? I would wonder. *Or maybe God made good rain and the devil made the bad storms. If that was the case, why did God make the devil in a way that he could become the devil in the first place?*

Junior high was teaching me about earthquakes, and lava, and typhoons that were hard to reconcile with what I knew of Jesus, and that's probably the year that I stopped sleeping. I'd lie awake in my bed at night feeling eight miles away from my parents' bedroom; eight miles between us that a fault line could rip right through. And I'd pray to always be safe, to always be spared.

Something inside—it seemed for all of my life—made me feel like I never quite understood how prayer worked *really*, because disasters were surely happening in places where I thought kids must certainly be praying similar prayers. It was far too much to stomach. I could not bear the thought of being so vulnerable, exposed, and unprotected. I could not bear the thought of anyone else being so either—from the storms, and the robbers who probably lurked outside my window, and the men with their knives and their twisted smiles that my grandmother's Lifetime movies suggested were out there just waiting for me to reach my college years. And yet, the contradictions were there, glaring at me from between the pews and the news every time I shut my eyes at night.

I would read Laura Ingalls Wilder books and Henry Blackaby devotions and watch *Bewitched* reruns each evening for hours just to distract myself from the fear that I constantly fought.

"Faith can move mountains," I'd repeat. "I can do all things through Christ who strengthens me and angels encamp around me." Envisioning celestial beings with their broad shoulders, large swords, and ever-watchful eyes that were just as greedy for my safety as I, I'd fall asleep.

I am safe because I believe that God keeps me safe.

I am not threatened by the storms.

They bring the flowers.

They bring the flowers.

They bring the flowers.

From within the crowd, stretching up on my tiptoes years before, I had begged Jesus to tell me how to live the most meaningful life. His answer, as I had understood it, was instructions on how to be a knower and a truster. But as I was getting older, knowing and trusting began to feel similar to perfecting the craft of ignoring; ignoring questions, contradictions, and that which did not apply to one's immediate situation though it may apply to another's; ignoring until you couldn't and then accepting your lot as it was because *this world was never your home in the first place.*

God would keep us safe and the storms would bring the flowers. But when they didn't, well, I guess they'd bring death. But death would bring heaven (for believers at least), and that was the goal all along. Heaven was a balm and a silencer for suffering. It was the glass half full of an otherwise terrifying reality. But it wasn't here; not yet.

Hamster Dentures

On more than one occasion, I was reprimanded for running— what the adults called—"my damn mouth." The only pink-slips and paddle-pops that I received during early high school came, not after toilet papering the teacher's room or removing tires from an enemy's car in the parking lot, but after my chatter could be tolerated no longer. Throughout my whole upbringing, I would rather die than get in trouble, and yet my damn mouth would compulsively throw me under the bus every *single* time. This was no truer than within the church walls.

My best friend Rebecca and I—even as we made our way into high school—would scribble on every single offering envelope within reach, filling them with dumb stories and questions about congregants' new teeth or loud snores. These small slips of paper bridled our vocal chords for a while. Until, that is, one of us would mention what it might look like if, say, that brand new set of teeth were to be worn in the mouth of a small animal, like perhaps the dancing hamsters from that one commercial.

The shoulder-shaking would ensue; and there is no panic like the Sunday Morning Shoulder Shake panic (except of course for the Sunday Morning Choir Loft Shoulder Shake Panic, which is by far the worst of the two). It was a dark path of uncontrollable, unstoppable laughter only magnified by the idea of being caught: the church giggles, some call them.

My parents, sitting half a pew down on yellowing cushions, rarely had to correct us seeing as how Rebecca's dad was our small church's pastor. And he had few qualms whatsoever with stopping a sermon dead in its tracks and staring us down until shame had ushered our chortles back into our ribs where they belonged.

"I'll wait," he'd say, destroying us both. I was always mortified when he'd blast us to pieces but also grateful, knowing I was near gone otherwise. How else might one come back down to earth once they've thought about a hamster with dentures too big for its face just as they were too big for Ms. Camp's?

In my recovery, I would stare at the stained glass in an effort to not glance back over at Rebecca who was always just that one glance away from catching the infectious shoulder shakes again. Because of this, those windows and their sun rays are seared into my memory: the royal blue robes that all the women around Jesus wore, the way they made the hay under the Baby Christ's body look comfortable, the regality of the tomb-side angel and how it appeared that he didn't have all that many social skills.

I was particularly fascinated with the red sun stuck in the sky above the crucified Jesus, both of them held in place by the mysterious stuff that keeps the glass together. It always looked like a Lifesaver to me.

One eye-shift away from the candy-colored star was the largest stained glass of them all, hovering right above the pulpit. Jesus, floating in what seemed to be rain, demonstrated the scars on his outwardly turned hands, expressionless. I thought about what it would be like to have him step through that glass, for heaven to be right behind the two-dimensional rain and not just at the end of our lives—that close.

But it wasn't. Rebecca and I had spent many "stay-in-the fellowship-hall-during-church-council" hours crawling through the warped wood and webs of the speaker-space behind the glass. Our scraped knees and made-up stories of hidden tunnels and secret lives offered us many exciting things, but heaven didn't seem to be one of them.

It was real, right? I'd wonder. *Just not here, not yet, right? Not in or behind this stained glass. Right. Not actually presently present . . . right . . .*

I'd wonder if this Jesus would ever care for me to do anything else with my life other than just wait to die and get people to think the correct thoughts in the meantime; if he might ask *anything* radical of me, because I was willing. I didn't just want to be a knower, a truster, an ignorer. I didn't just want to be a verse-memorizer, answer-giver, hell-avoider.

I needed him to be much more than two-dimensional because of how it made me worry that my life would be two-dimensional as well—this life that I had given to him when I hoped that he would be biggest, and best, and most. Religion felt boring and inconsistent, the opposite of challenging. It was old liturgies written by someone who had died decades before and homilies that seemed quite unspecific. It was being fourteen, and saying generic prayers at night, missing the magic of childhood, and searching for it in old speaker-spaces.

A faint thud would jar me out of my stained-glass study, and I'd look down to see a crumpled envelope resting beside my thigh, two feet from its former owner who was one shoulder shake away from combusting into thin air.

As the worship services would wrap, we'd make the same Sunday morning ride home that I'd made with my folks my whole life. And I'd mull over the dullness that was the life of a person of God. It was gloomy: void of energy, vibrancy, and fullness. This purpose to which I had dedicated myself when I asked as the seeker, *what must I do?*, seemed like little more than a hall pass keeping me on heaven's good list on the chance that a tornado or Lacy's dumb driving would take me from this world and on into the next. It didn't feel like a terrible thing to have, but it also didn't feel like the greatest life in this world to live. I was ready to reconsider Christianity as just another part of me that I'd inherited from my folks—like reflux, or brown eyes, or grass allergies.

And I may very well have done just that if the Baptists hadn't come around.

2

Revivals and Rules

The Priest

You must stay cautious, but there's a lot on your mind. You're replaying each step of the rituals you recently finished performing at the temple and hoping to God that you did them well (or at least appeared to). A lot of people depend on your actions, your choices, and your image. The pressure is unique as you are unique.

"Keep your wits about you," reminds your inner coach. These roads and these parts are for the thems and those. And you work really hard to not be counted among them.

Up ahead, the sight of which wriggles and blends with the waves of the day's heat, a figure lies doubled over and contorted. Quickly checking behind and in front, you gather your robe-bottom to cross the road within enough yards that it doesn't seem too obvious as to why. Your time and your purity are precious and "for the people." Both could not afford to be wasted on whatever this is.

Some olive branches rustle, and you allow them to turn your gaze upward as you pass the body.

Look away, disassociate, walk quickly ahead to your holy obligations. The people . . . the people are waiting.

And watching.

I See that Hand

WHEN JIM BEAM (YEP, you read that right) came to town, it was as if everyone's dry bones just started jigging around. He was a local revival preacher with a drawn out "y'all," and he had a redeemed, racy past, so people trusted him. His methods were impassioned and persuasive. And though I'd later hear them be called "revival scare-tactics," with them he could get the most devout church elder to rethink his salvation, the most rough and tumble agnostic to walk the aisle.

"If you could just get a sinner to Jim, he'd change his mind," they'd say.

I was fifteen and the proud new owner of a learner's driving permit. I'd practice the art of four-way stops while taxiing my mom around our 2,500-person community to pick up sliced turkey and prescriptions. In these small-town stores where every bell-ring of the front door was like an episode of *Cheers*, gossip of who had finally, *actually*, come to the Lord was whirling around like the long awaited cool air of fall at the end of a sticky summer.

"I sure did think she was already saved," I'd hear regularly.

"Well, she is now for sure, Bev, so praise God."

I'd seen this passion in mere flashes before, primarily beaming out of older, tired faces during Christmas and Easter performances when it seemed like those over the age of forty would come out of their Holy Spirit hibernation. *Christ is risen! He is risen indeed!* I loved and hated this zeal for its predictable rareness. A faith that came with consistent energy sounded nice, I'd think. And it sounded like one might be coming our way.

Our town's residents had traveled many miles in caravans over the previous months to get their people within earshot of Jim's microphone. Now, he was here, on their turf, in their house, ready to do God's business. I'd shown up, semi-skeptically, in my school uniform after ball practice to see what all the fuss was about and to sit with my friends who'd included me among their "three people to invite." But I was curious. *Why were the adults so awake? What had lit their fire?*

The testimony shared was unbelievably riddled with chaos and bad choices. All of the major three were covered (drugs, sex, alcohol), which made me insecure about my own uneventful story. Good girls were not great candidates for offering crowd-transforming testimonies, I was gathering. This was unfortunate since crowd-transforming testimonies were becoming such a commodity at the time.

"Well, my parents wouldn't hurry up one day after church, and so I prayed that God would save my soul in our minivan," I'd rehearse. It was hardly the sanctified cocaine binges and orgies that laced the redemption stories of movement-leaders (something I was so interested in becoming).

But the roads of movement leaders seemed to lead to the same destination: repentance and purity. Somewhere along their paths, these revival preachers learned the rules after God had brought them out of their rule-breaking and taught them how to live their lives clean and clear of rule-breakers. I figured it was fine enough that I skipped a step, forewent the rule-breaking, and moved right onto the faithfulness of rule-keeping. The priest in me was being born.

My heart loudly whomped around my torso during the invitation time, which always followed directly after the sing-song production of the sermon. It would be hard for one's heart not to do so if you were even remotely paying attention. There was a science to revival preaching: energizing music, risqué stories from one's wildest years, miraculous spiritual healing and personal prosperity, a reminder of the threats in this world, and an invitation to accept Jesus.

I wondered if anyone close to me could hear the inside of my chest as I reminded myself that I didn't need saving again. *I didn't need saving again.* The bottom of First Baptist Church—and the top—were packed with short, teased, hair-sprayed perms and the overalls who had driven them there. The youth filled the front rows allowing the whole room to look upon the next generation of followers. The lights were all on because this was before lights started to be turned off during church.

The baptistry waters were risen and warmed, just in case. Somewhere in a Sunday school room in the back, a stack of Bibles and commitment cards had been organized and the deacons trained to pass them out. It was nothing like Sunday mornings, though Sunday mornings would try their hardest to replicate it all. Revival nights were close-quarters, listening ears, there by passion and not obligation. They had a mystical element to them. And it was relieving to think that maybe somewhere deep down the general public wanted a thrilling and mystical element to life as much as I did.

"God is telling me to tell you that someone in here could be hit by a car when they leave this building tonight. They could have a heart attack the moment they get home. Don't miss your chance, church," he'd croon. "God is asking for your soul. He wants to set you free!" Pastor Beam was grooming the crowd for commitments. I sat back, trying to remain confident in my own story.

I do not need saving again. I don't need saving again, my spirit attempted to calm itself with logic. The pianist circled back around to the first verse of "I Surrender All."

"There are some of you who have been in hiding with your double life, and you need to make that right today. Confess your sins and be healed! There are some of you who think that you've been in good standing with the Lord, but your current life has been all about your good works while your eternal life is headed straight to hell. Just lift that hand. All heads are bowed, and all eyes are closed. Just lift that hand if you need prayer. I see that hand. I see that hand. Ma'am, I see you . . ."

I am saved. I believe in Jesus. I don't need saving again.

"I'm sorry folks, I know y'all have to get home, but God has told me that there is someone here tonight that is just moments away from making a decision. And God is gracious enough to give them a little more time to work up the bravery to handle their sin. So we'll do the same. C'mon, let me see the hand of the person who is hesitating. God is calling you tonight! God wants you to really give your life to him tonight!"

Before my lungs could fully crawl out of my throat, my hand was raised and shaking. I thought I'd been saved, but I could be so wrong. I hadn't broken any rules, but maybe I also didn't know all of the rules. And I couldn't afford to be incorrect with how fragile our earthly lives were, we'd been reminded.

"I see you. I see you. I see that hand," others had joined me. *Who could they all be?*

"Now put your hands down, and everyone open your eyes. Can I just ask those who raised their arms to be brave enough to come on down and pray the Sinner's Prayer with us? Let us circle around you and celebrate you as a part of the family! Come on down, my sisters; come on down, my brother. Come on down, you who are scared. Jesus said, 'Whoever disowns me before others, I will disown before my Father in heaven.' Let's not be in the business of disowning tonight, y'all. Be proud of your salvation! Be proud of your Lord!"

My knees creaked into a stand faster than I could decide for them to. All my guts had subconsciously realized that there would be no retreating once the hand-counting ushers (friends of my parents) had seen mine extend. My soul was getting reborn again, alongside the souls of fourteen other churchgoers, a few unchurched people, and the youth pastor. I'd doubly believed; I'd been doubly saved.

And though I felt manipulated, I didn't care. Something like zealousness had been in the room that night. Something like purpose, thrill in spirit and air in lungs, had come between those walls, and a whole group of people had experienced it. With the question for Jesus, *what must I do, teacher?*, still drumming in my head, I wondered if maybe I was glimpsing a better version of the answer.

To love God and my neighbor was to be a part of a movement that passionately brought sinners out of their hushed and wicked ways and into the world of big testimony. To love God and my neighbor meant to live a life of clean hands and a pure heart, not associating with our old selves or the toxic and tempting ways of the wicked.

I was stepping into the role of the first-century Jewish priest in the story of the Good Samaritan who was bound by the law to not meddle with dead things unless he was to be taken out of his normal routine of service and thrown into the meticulous purity rituals of body-cleansing. I was not only concluding that to keep oneself worthy and righteous was to accept the grace of being spared by Jesus's blood, but was to also teach this truth to others and dedicate myself to not coming near the impurities of what (or who) looked like death.

To compromise was not an option now, said this culture, said Jim. This was an expectation to which I could rise. This was not a bored or stagnant faith. Rather, it had a role in the real lives of people, which was, namely, to keep them clean and to ensure that they were heaven-bound.

I was so glad to be growing in some version of Christianity that required something of the world that I didn't even care that I'd been lumped into the number of recent souls won that evening.

"I sure did think you were already saved," they'd say to my face.

"Well, she is now for sure, Bev, so praise God."

Religion vs. Relationship

As a freshman, I'd just started to wrap all of my free mind-time around both the idea of movement-making and the idea of finding a nice "man of God" to marry (or at least with whom to go to prom). So when my friends from the Baptist Church—who were still riding the Jim Beam high—asked me to accompany them to a youth conference in Memphis, I accepted the last spot in the van enthusiastically like I'd been invited onto a dating show.

The auditorium at the conference was darker, colder, more packed than any congregational space of which I'd ever been a part. I detangled my mustard seed necklace and wrote down quotes in my Mede notebook like the rest of our group (all sporting their identical "non-conformist" T-shirts).

I was learning that the Baptists were a different breed than people with whom I was used to holding religious company. They were the confident theologians, the Bible drill competitors, the ones who knew exactly where to find the Scriptures on why we shouldn't marry outside of our own race. The Baptists had answers. They knew why it was important to walk well the straight and narrow, how to love our neighbors by getting them saved while not getting too close to the dirty details of their lives. And I was the Methodist who had memorized the doxology and a good deal of VBS one-liners, but who still depended heavily on the Table of Contents for my Scripture reading.

The gap in my knowledge of the book that was supposed to sustain our lives compared to that of the Baptists made me nervous about being found out during our travels. Before leaving, I took the teal Bible I'd received at the end of Confirmation Class and began to massage its binding, highlighting any passages that seemed significant enough. I peeled two Kodak photos off of my decoupaged bedroom door and stuck them inside the Old and New Testaments where they looked like natural place holders for the daily reading that was obviously taking place. And I patted myself on the back, and said, "Now that's a used Bible."

I blended nicely, I thought as I glanced around the room. To the left was my most recent crush. To the right was the guest speaker who was in the middle of telling a traumatizing story about two girls getting kidnapped, raped, and shot, and how that pertained to why we shouldn't listen to music with curse words in it. In the back, Sonicflood played worship music while the words "Religion vs. Relationship" appeared on the screen. And the invitation followed for the predictable trifecta of response: salvation, rededication, and the call to ministry.

The music, and lights, and soft-spoken prayers made my body feel like it wanted to move, *again*. That word *relationship* in regards to Jesus made me feel like I could melt on into my own soul. *Being in love with God:* I had never heard this sentiment before. I needed it. I needed to leave my newly worn Bible on the plush, theater-style seats and walk through the smoky room down to the altar where I could tell God that I didn't just want to be righteous like the priest because I was intimate with rules but because I was intimate with the divine. That felt sustainable and maybe universal. That felt like something worthy of aisle-walking. But among the multiple-choices for why one might leave their seat, "declaring love for God" didn't seem to be among them.

Salvation isn't how I'm to respond now, I thought, *even though, there goes that youth director, right on down the aisle again.* I'd "been saved" for years, I hadn't forgotten; and I'd even been re-saved since to make it super official. Seeing as how I'd never even held a boy's hand, I assumed I didn't need to rededicate in the ways that the kids who frequented the the backroads were rededicating (though apparently I was obliged to get rid of some of my CDs upon returning home, lest I be kidnapped).

This left only the call to ministry, which felt *not wrong*. It felt not entirely incorrect for this seeker-turned-priest to make a public declaration affirming that I had indeed heard Jesus when he told us what to do. I had only ever thought about possibly being an artist or a writer, and even those were loose goals. So if God wanted to pay me for being extra-faithful, extra-called, then I wasn't going to stand in his way by staying put in my comfortable seat.

Though it felt mildly restricted, I closed my eyes and walked the aisle one more time. I wanted to be *in love with God,* as they were saying. I wanted a Holy Spirit that didn't just peek its head out at revivals. I wanted a faith that was relational, important, intimate, and unique. I wanted there to be a God who felt close, a God who had placed a special calling just on my life, a God who wanted me to live in a very challenging and specific way and wanted my friends to do the same.

My knees hit the kneeling pillow, and I started to cry thinking about how this might be the moment to which I would trace back from my future as a preacher, or a youth director, or a missionary.

I'd barely gotten one deep breath in at the altar when I was whisked away to a room with cards and counselors.

"Welcome to the family," they said. I grinned in silence, weary of getting saved and wishing that there had been a place on the paper to write what I thought I was experiencing—a place to write that I'd said yes to a vocational life of clean hands, a pure heart, and the teaching of the importance of both because of my new and deep friendship with God.

But faithfulness was not so varied.

Two Lives

"Watch this," she said, with that tone of instigation that was never too far from her lips.

"Are you going to buy me a promise ring, Daddy? You know, so I won't just go around having sex with all the boys? As if a ring could hold me back, Daddy. You know I'm going to give you trouble!" she laughed. He rolled his eyes and went back to his paper. I melted into a pubescent puddle of *Oh, God.* Why were Lacy and I still friends?

I wanted to evaporate in the same way I wanted to evaporate when any immature sixteen-year-old would go around the lunch table at school asking all those standing near about their first kisses and periods; in the same way I wanted to evaporate when a romantic scene would come on the TV at home in our living room full of people and I'd become mortified at the thought of someone watching me watching it. Me, with a mind beyond its years and a body embarrassed of its own existence because of how susceptible it was to knocking me off the straight and narrow.

The world around sex seemed so foreign and not yet for me. There were so many rules to follow when it came to Jesus and bodies: rules about bathing suit cuts, and who we could and couldn't ride in cars with, and what we were to save for when. It made everything that had to do with sexuality feel line-crossing, which just made me anxious in ways that I thought we all should be anxious. *Weren't we all anxious?*

I'd never heard of a promise (or purity) ring before, but it sounded like the kind of thing I'd be into, being a "priest" and all. It sounded like it would naturally complement the purity books that I was devouring at the time in an effort to make sense of all the scary changes and choices starting to take place among my friends. Whatever sex actually was, it made me feel young and nervous. So in a public display of conviction, I requested a promise ring as a gift one Christmas that I might join all of my other dedicated (and rededicated) priestly friends in the fight against our own defiant pants. I'd decided not to have sex before marriage, out of fear of falling from grace and as to maintain a clean-as-snow testimony for my one-day husband.

A year later, a guy I'd gotten to know started giving me rides home from town on account of my being lately bloomed, which brought me into the tenth grade still without a license (and still having not been kissed despite hours of pining and prayer). We'd met through sports, bonded over church, shared a mutual friend circle and a mutual affection for ministry.

I felt gauchely tall in the middle seat of his old truck, anchored only by the confident hand on my left thigh meant to steady me, or something. We'd ride without speaking as we listened to R&B music and made out at stop signs in the dark. It wasn't quite the courting and the boundaries of common respect that I'd hoped to preserve. But it could get there, I thought, finding myself lost in and put out by Scripture's lack of specificity regarding something as consequential as high school relationships.

A quiz on the internet—which was made possible by a dial-up cable connected to a clunky Dell computer in my parents' room—labeled my ability to flirt "appalling and nonexistent." Never riding the waves of the charming, coy center, my attempts at stirring attraction were limited to the extremes: appearing either like an apathetic friend-zoner or an aggressive tease who had no clue that the quips she was dishing could have so many sexual implications.

"Oh, you have no idea what I'm capable of," I said in an instance of the latter one day outside of the baseball field. The words, haphazardly chosen as a rebuttal to a joke made about my good-girl prudence sent a charge through his face that caused him to grab both of my hands in public. The good girl status wasn't good for testimonies or for getting boyfriends, I'd determined. At least joking about a bad girl status could conjure a reaction.

Immediately, I felt so very on his radar and so very nervous that he might one day try to cash in on that ridiculously empty insinuation. *But he wouldn't, right? We were all waiting because of God and our testimonies, right? And in six years when we were married, if we were married, we could make good on it then, right? Surely anything that eluded to sex among my church friends was just line-skirting jokes, right?* Otherwise, I'd understood something very incorrectly.

Sixty minutes later, I stared down the neglected edges of a grassy pipeline that I'd never noticed on our many drives home before. The dirt clouds from his truck brakes weren't acting near enough like curtains for the daytime hour. The leather seats were hardly a honeymoon bed. My school uniform looked like a sadder version of the white gown that I had imagined.

"How do you want to do this?" he said, hand, thigh, steadied, "Do we need protection?"

I continued staring—confused, giddy, sick. I thought about how fast, one way or the other, the last few years were about to just go away and how long they'd taken to get there. I thought about the story about my relationship that I wanted to tell my future kids and my future congregants and how this felt like an account that I didn't love. I thought about my squeaky clean testimony and how this could scuff it a bit like Jim Beam's, but also there was something about knowing right and choosing wrong *after* you'd accepted the call to ministry that just felt especially heretical.

I thought about my damn mouth and how it had gotten us here in the first place like the ignorant traitor that it was. I thought about my supply of right and wrong answers, all those who might hear about this and be influenced by my actions, the fact that I didn't want to have to walk another aisle again for something so uncommitted. *And*, I guessed, if I had any capability and desire at all to do differently, I probably should, since that kind of sobriety probably didn't come around all too often in pipeline situations such as these with guys so attractive and hormones so unwieldy.

"I think I gave you the wrong idea," I said eventually, deflating. "Can you take me home?" Respectfully, he did, and was kind enough to give me a few more rides over the next couple of weeks before cutting off communication.

"A Proverbs 31 woman, Scripture says, honors her husband throughout her *whole* life, not just the days after she meets him," a minister's wife told me soon after, attempting to soothe the blow of a fling now foiled by reminding me that somewhere out in the world was a young man who would fit the bill of every quality I ever wanted; and I was already to be honoring him now; and I already had by not letting things progress with this other guy. It's odd, isn't it? That in no other relationship do we encourage children to make magic lists of sinless people and then to wait on them. We don't embolden young folks to decide what they need, as if they are rubbing magic lamps, and to hold their breaths until a flawless best friend, or business partner, or mentor comes around. Yet, this was normal, throughout many of my years and for many of my friends who were juggling the disappointments of adolescent dating (or lack thereof): *write down what you want, and wait.* It took me years to unlearn the toxic, fairytale prophecies of those who were trying to teach a Christian sexual and relational ethic with just one narrative that many of them had rarely witnessed or experienced themselves.

Meanwhile, I missed the thrill, and I felt lonely in the promises to priestly purity that I thought we'd all made together. I wondered if shrewdness in sanctuaries but limitlessness in truck cabs was a bigger reality for more people than I realized. Did everyone have a hidden part of their life, one for which the God switch periodically got turned off? Secular and sacred as categories into which we were to divide our thoughts, our music, and our experiences made me feel like a soul torn. And I really just wanted to be whole. I really just wanted all of us to be whole.

Women in the Bible

"I told my dad what you said about what you wanted to be when you grow up," spouted my friend. It was 2004, and I had already begun to send in applications to schools that would prepare me for seminary.

"Oh yeah?" I asked, confused about why it mattered. "What'd he say?"

"He said that it would not be right for you to become a pastor. Women aren't supposed to preach; it's pretty clear in the Bible. He said it would be disobedient to God." I recognized his zeal. It was the same fervor that had laced my own words for years. He was trying to save me.

"That doesn't sound right," I spouted. It surely didn't feel right. I'd done a lot of work, and learned a lot of answers, and could wield my decently loud mouth when I needed to for God. I'd established an on-campus Christians' club for teenagers who were interested in skipping lunch to pray, co-created several regional youth rallies to bring revival back into our wayward school halls, convinced our student council to show a screening of *The Passion of Christ* during Holy Week, passed home-burned CDs chock full of Christian rap out to dozens of annoyed classmates during recess.

I'd spent the night at friends' houses so that we could sneak out and anonymously hang homemade signs at the football field reading, "God ~~Wuz~~ Is Here." I'd given sermons, in front of men in fact. I'd led worship with bands, and learned the art of the poetic prayer-pause, and figured out how to make a darn good flyer for a Jesus event. And, here he was—the son of a deacon whose church had taken me to the next level of my faith—telling me that if I wanted to be obedient to God, I would not become a preacher.

"I don't think that's true," I bit back. "He must have read it wrong."

Rushing home, I tore open my Bible (now genuinely worn) and searched in the sections that my friend had referenced. I read and reread. And reread and reread.

And lo and behold, he was right.

"Women should be silent in the churches. For they are not permitted to speak, but should be subordinate, as the law also says." It was there in 1 Corinthians, the answer, glaring at me and anxiously awaiting my decision to believe it or to not.

Over the course of the next year, I dropped the conflict between my inner-gut and my reading-eyes on the doorstep of any respectable adult who might listen.

"Some people say that those instructions were relevant to the culture at the time," my parents offered.

"I know what Paul says, but the Bible goes on to say that there's no longer male, female, Jew or Greek," my pastor's wife assured. "Plus some of the earliest church leaders, like Priscilla and Aquila, were women. I can't imagine that they were very silent."

I realize now that my spiritual turbulence had far less to do with the actual words that I'd read and rather had more to do with the fact that my once black-and-white Bible now had some gray, some tension. Up to this point, all of the rebuttals for life's problems could be located like in a handbook without (admitted) contradiction or confusion.

Now, owning and celebrating what I thought was my calling and what I knew were my gifts would be synonymous with welcoming a wrench in my understanding of Scripture. I'd been working so diligently for so long at keeping my robe clean and wisely located on the road's less contaminated side, and now I was being told that it was never my robe to begin with. Only men wear the robes of the priest.

The system of answers I'd clung to so tightly and held over the heads of my peers so heavily, at the very least, were now causing me pain and rejection. The system of answers that the believers believed, to which I'd dedicated my entire self, were being understood by some in such a way that left me less room at a table that I thought had been built for me.

Me: raised in a home of country folk and devout Methodists who believed men could cook the gumbo and women could shoot the deer, and we would all learn to handle a bull, and clean a fish, and get a four-wheeler out of the mud since the load takes all the hands at one point or another. Me: who had known and loved women pastors—good ones, kind ones, competent ones. Me: who had been primarily shaped by the faith of women friends.

I'll avoid it, I concluded, tapping into those familiar habits of ignoring while wondering what other leadership roles I could take on without dealing with the issue of debatable defiance. And like a good Southern woman's understanding of political talk, I logged these arguable Scriptures into a file of what not to discuss. They were distracting kindling for a time-wasting flame, and there was so much I could be doing with or without ordination, surely. In that instance, right-knowing became something to piece together, something for which to learn proper etiquette, something that good people disagreed on in their efforts to get each other living the life that God desired.

Therefore, right-knowing became a structure on which I could not hang the hat of my whole spirituality; and though I'd never say it out loud, I would need to discover another version, a different comprehension of what it meant to love God with everything and love my neighbor as myself in order to keep walking.

Providentially, college would be a perfectly odd place for such uncovering.

3

Grace and Truth (but Mostly Truth)

The Levite

As his cloak disappears into the distance ahead of you, a small sigh of both relief and annoyance escapes your nostrils. How fast he scurries off to his next obligation. You dodged a bullet, you think, by not following the professional path of the priest.

Life in your current lane holds much less pressure, many more normal people with their normal existences; many more normal people that get left behind in his temple dust, whom you linger back to serve in God's name.

Ah, but that's ok, you admit. He can have that life. This one of yours may not be the ladder-top of religious authority for which you assumed your special calling had destined you; but it did come with a lot less expectation, a lot more freedom, and a lot fewer eyes on your actions.

In this version of you, you're liberated to know and champion right belief on your terms and to serve Levi's tribe without the whole wide world looking to your every move. You find this lack of scrutiny aids in your own judgmental eye, which likely makes you better company.

The recollection of this liberty puts a pep in your step, and you find yourself almost dancing down the dirt path—almost. But then, startled, your fluttering feet come to a halt a mere three yards before the body of the bandit-beaten victim. The breath you were inhaling has been sucked right on out of you since this is not a scene you've gotten used to or anything.

What do you do?

What do you do?

What in God's name do you do? You search your mind for tools, your peripheral for assistance.

You know the law, but you also know that far less is on the line if you break it than it would be for some—than it would be for the one walking up ahead. But drawing near to dying things like this would be highly inconvenient and highly frowned upon. Just because your heart is softer than it once was doesn't mean there is any less conflict within you. It doesn't make the rules less important.

What would the priest do?, you brood. What did the priest do?, you remember.

And in no time at all, you're following in his footsteps. But, though your feet and your mind are resolved enough to move along, your eyes have yet to catch up. A half mile past the body, you stumble over into your own tears. How will you ever resolve the war between the changing spirit within you, the needs of those around you, and the authority on which you've always relied?

Chapel Confessions

"I WANT YOU TO imagine that your head is being cut open right now," my professor, an atheist, instructed. "Now visualize me unpacking all the things you've been spoon-fed about your faith all these years and replacing them with well-informed, educated, open-minded content. You will not leave here with the same faith with which you first came, I can promise you that," he threatened.

Challenge accepted, asshole, I stewed, immediately feeling guilty for the sentiment that had so effortlessly overtaken my brain.

My small, Methodist-affiliated college was a red-brick campus that existed a short fifty minutes away from my parents' house. There, you could find 900 students and not one Christian Studies program if your life depended on it. And mine had felt like it had the moment I realized I would not be receiving enough scholarship money to attend the Baptist university in Nashville on which I had so set my sights. Begrudgingly accepting second best, I settled for a Religious Studies degree taught by an instructor who didn't know or love the son of God as the way, the truth, and the life.

"She got the ribbons out, again," I winced while on a phone-call to tell my pastor back home how very bizarre my college experience was turning out to be. "Why would a grown woman be in a unitard during worship, and what does it have to do with being in love with Jesus?"

"Welcome to the Methodist Church," he said, tongue in cheek. He was Methodist, but more Baptist-Methodist than Presbyterian-Methodist; and there was a difference.

"I swear, they worship more activists than they do God around here. It's felt like, since I arrived, there's been this underlying liberal agenda in every discussion. No emotionally charged worship service, only older songs with the lights on, a few sung in Spanish (as if any of us knows Spanish). There was a big presentation about Native Americans and also a lesbian got up and talked about a seminary in Colorado. If I hear one more person pray to 'the One we each call Holy,' I'm going to vomit. If this is what college is going to be like, I cannot wait for these next few years to go ahead and pass on by so that I can get on with the life I know I've been called to live."

The Christianity of liberal arts higher education felt initially and primarily so formless and up for anyone's interpretation. The faith that called itself faith in college looked highly distracted by subversive politics and the on-edgeness of always having to be politely PC. I thought that this version of Jesus-following looked an awful lot like the world around it; and I was not there to be a part of the world. It would take me a long time—a long, long time— to recognize these understandings and practices as respectable options for faithfulness. It would take me a long time to not be so afraid of more opened doors (or so annoyed by those words alone), of realizing that I'd not been asked to guard them much less lock or mock them in the first place.

We'd just gotten back from choir camp, a boot-camp week to learn a year's worth of songs put on by the organization that would fund most of my tuition and take up most of my time over the next few years. My roommate, whose Facebook profile led me to believe that she would be a trustworthy ally in the (conservative) faith, rowed beside me on gym equipment after my New Testament class, educating me on the sexual orientation of all the attractive men in our seventy-person singing group.

"Him too?"

"Him too."

"That's a lot of guys who like guys . . ."

"There are a lot of guys who like guys, Britney."

"I've never met one before now . . ."

"You've met one before now."

It felt near impossible to wrap my mind around how I could even start to belong in a place like this. It was not a ship being run as I would run a ship, as the people that I called my people would run ships, as the people who I thought loved God most would run ships. *Anyone* could give the devotion at the weekly worship service despite their choices in romantic partners or how *gone* they'd gotten at the sorority party the weekend before. Anyone could be a leader in choral groups, and student government, and religious life. Anyone could be anyone that they wanted to be, except for closed-minded, of course, which is what I began to feel like my convictions had been labeled.

Believe what you want, think what you want, love who you want, become what you want. Just don't let that be traditional or right-wing.

"They're preaching open-mindedness with minds that are closed to me and people like me!" I screamed through the phone along with a string of other aggressive comments about not being in Tennessee. "All thoughts and beliefs are acceptable unless they're conservative. Diversity is encouraged as a way to include people from all perspectives except for mine."

I was not used to being anything resembling the minority (which I was still a long way away from being). I was not used to processing any form of discrimination (realistic or not) on truly any scale outside of my womanism, which I didn't even recognize yet. But instead of being able to see this as an opportunity to relate to others who had felt excluded, instead of seeing my own contributions to said exclusion, I counted it as martyrdom and read Scripture after Scripture about persecution and fire.

"You're Baptist, right?" they'd ask with a dab of insult. "No, Methodist," I'd respond with a dab of pride for being mistaken as a person who honored Scripture.

"I would have sworn you were Baptist . . ."

With belief still functioning as my marker for faithfulness, qualifications for community then depended on who agreed with what. During many years of junior high and high school, what deemed people eligible for being my close friends were their postures towards alcohol and sex. If you were waiting or waiting again, then we understood each other enough to move forward. But, with the submergence into the world of sexual acceptance, that litmus-blue soon became the response for how one did or did not view homosexuality.

Jane's van, a hand-me-down from her Arkansas parents, looked like something your old aunt might drive. It's back-end door needed all of one's extra body weight to shut, and it sported a bumper sticker that read, "Have a Rice Day." We'd been asked to be counselors for a high school retreat at a church outside of the city. She picked me up in the Religious Studies parking lot one Friday after class.

Her hair in pigtails, tie-dyed shirt slightly hidden by the nineties overalls, and the well-known reputation for being so friendly that people assumed she must do drugs, all prompted a general bafflement within me. I had a lot of questions for a person so hard to label. In which box did she fit? Mine or theirs? Would we be friends? Or would I have to mask my beliefs out of fear that she would label them bigoted?

We remember this part differently. I feel as though I surely conjured up some small talk to ease us into business. She says that it was as if the first thing out of my mouth when the door closed was, "So what do you believe about homosexuality?" I don't recall how she answered, but it must have been comforting enough since we became the best of friends who would soon be growing the pack of people with whom we'd surround ourselves over the next three years—banded together by causes common enough for it to feel like home to me.

They called us the God Squad, and I wore it like oppression as I sat in the courtyard of Cline Hall waiting on my clothes to dry, highlighting Bible verses while doing my nightly devotional. Drunk frat boys would stumble into our coed space and dive into theological discussions they'd never remember the next day; and I'd note my opportunities for bearing witness to people who were "filling their God-sized hole with the things of this world."

I talked about school like it was a flame that was refining me, testing my will to stay steadfast. And I flocked to people who prioritized quiet times, held each other accountable for masturbating, and wanted to spend hours breaking into the locked chapel to sing out our love for God together between midterms.

We'd found each other in our searching for theological common ground, meaning, spiritual connection, and authentic (sans unitards and ribbons) worship. Each Thursday night at nine o'clock, we'd gather so that we might light candles, curl up at the altar, and pray. It was here that our friendships melded, I think— here where we shared almost every single part of ourselves by way of something new we were discovering called confession.

What counted as porn?

When was it considered an eating disorder?

When was it considered depression?

· *Did the Bible really say you can't be with a man?*

Did the Bible really say you can't preach as a woman?

Are sleeping pills an idol if you can't see your life without them?

How far is too far with your girlfriend?

Is doubt wrong?

Is cussing bad?

At what point is alcohol destructive?

What does it mean to be called by God?

Can ministry be anything you do?

How do we heal from our parents' divorces?

How do we not be so afraid of divorcing as well?

Is there really a stark line between sacred and secular?

Who else has experienced abuse?

When will we see revival in this place?

I became a new person as trusted people listened and, without impulse to humiliate or necessarily advise, also shared in a way that people share when they have been cut off from their familiar upbringings and launched into new worlds. Confession within safe spaces was being marked by the ripple effect it was causing. Emotional healing was happening in real time with every *me too* that was spoken.

I was learning that there would always exist a comatose level of me so long as my life wasn't being shared in its specifics, in the uncut and unedited, whole version of itself. I was learning that there was no comparison between the damage that our choices or struggles cause and the damage that our loneliness in those choices and struggles cause—that the hiding is what kills us and the sharing what frees us. I was proud to be the Levite: still concerned with morality, but not so concerned about existing without imperfection that it kept me from relating to real people with real struggles like it had when I was the priest.

My first sense of committed community formed in those late-night chapel years. I'd felt the power of finding a group of people you can call yours—people who hear and pray—and then giving them your whole self without curation or shame. And I'd been introduced to the notion that maybe everyone has a little bit of curation they're dealing with. Maybe that crap was ok if we could be honest about it, if we wanted to get better together. Maybe—as the Levite within me was adopting—loving my neighbor was much less about us all knowing and doing right and much more about us all being honest about what we didn't know and what we hadn't done and then committing to figuring it out together.

There was still a goal that included spiritual healing, right practice, less brokenness in sexual and substance-ridden sin. But it didn't have to be mastered on the front side of friendship. We could do it hand in hand, if we would do it hand in hand.

Qualifying Grace

And with time and exposure (two of my most loyal nurses), I began to learn how to be acquaintances with people who thought and lived differently than I did. This was promising, since I had seen the power of what could happen when friends who thought the same got close and honest. It made me wonder if a more approachable and available posture would provide me a foot in the door for winning people over to the camp of righteousness, of full life.

Of course, it was their initiative that got the ball rolling. People who have been outsiders are so good at reaching out to those who feel (legitimately or not) like outsiders. It was their jokes, their hugs, their relentless interest in me as a person despite how open I was to the idea of judging and converting them, that began to warm my soul right on up to a place I didn't think that it could get.

The slips of tongue and twisted humor about black, brown, and gay people that would happen back in my hometown began to feel slightly and increasingly offensive. These folks now had names, faces, hands that swiped cafeteria cards for my meals when I forgot my own. Few of them fit the caricatures that had been assigned to them in the banter that bounced at their expense. Most were just looking for safe places to ask the same questions that I was asking about them. At the risk of "sounding like yet another moral-bending progressive imposing my expectations of political correctness," I began to respond to the punch-lines and insults with a diluted, disapproving chuckle.

"Hey now," I'd laugh, "those are my classmates you're talking about," my neck tightening at the thought of the conversation ever being overheard by an actual human in reference.

But reconciling my new friendships with my old everything was no easy task. I felt as if I was trying, similar to Amy Poehler's character in the movie *Mean Girls*, to be "the cool Christian," except one who was always having to revisit, refigure, and repaint whatever line I was refusing to cross at the time. Zero kindness or connection at all felt un-relational and wide of the mark—*Jesus did care for these people, in fact.* And I liked them. But too much kindness or connection (without disclaimer) felt like it could place me in dangerous territory of looking accepting. And acceptance was not the same as love; and love would not let people live in sin. I took on the outlook of loving the sinner while hating the sin as a means of coping and as a means of labeling my stance so that every conversation and every relationship might be filtered through it. But let me tell you something about loving the sinner while hating the sin: it is exhausting.

Books helped some to give me language that I could lean into when my interactions became heavy and confusing with the Levite's task of making sure that people understood that I both cared about them *and* had issues with their issues. Books about the codependence of compassion with challenge—namely, Randy Alcorn's *The Grace and Truth Paradox*—became staples that I couldn't keep on my shelf for very long as I insisted that person after person own a copy.

"The Word became flesh and made his dwelling among us. We have seen his glory, the glory of the one and only Son, who came from the Father full of grace and truth," my new literature would highlight in the first chapter of John as it warned against graceless truth and truthless grace. Without truth, it insisted, grace would fail to give us the structure that we needed to be better. Without grace, truth would fail to give us the room for error that we required as intrinsically sinful beings.

Balance became a gigantic word for my theology and for my understanding of "what I must do" when it came to loving my neighbor and existing faithfully in God's world.

Grace was making friends with people who made wrong choices. Truth was making sure our friendship was a means to an end and that that end was freedom from that which enslaved them. Sure, without grace—without compassion and a gentle smile—truth failed. It prevented us from holding company with those who so needed healing. But without truth—without clear rules and instructions—grace also failed. It permitted us to fall into the chasm it was trying to bridge in the first place.

The concept was revolutionary, giving justification to my feelings and to the place beyond which I just was not ready to move. It gave me an appreciation for the idea of balance and for how one might live a life in both relationship and accountability.

So grace and truth (but mostly truth) became my religion. Or maybe more accurately, relationships with regulations did. We were to be like Jesus, and Jesus generously spoke to the woman at the well while also instructing her to go and sin no more. Life was only half full if we were extending kindness without sharing the behavior expectations that might set people free. And I would not be caught in cowardice, allowing the friends that I loved to live half-lives dictated by their vices.

However, holding the correct level of tension was burdensome, often dramatic, and frequently intertwined with disappointment when someone I'd loved to freedom dipped back into the pool of their "bad choices." It became overwhelming to pray *again* for someone to miraculously begin loving the opposite sex, overwhelming to be reprimanded by college leadership for encouraging such unfair expectations, overwhelming to ride the rollercoaster of friends returning back to me when they were choosing what I approved of and disappearing again when they weren't.

I was just starting to wonder if the reign-holding of sinner-love/sin-hate was above my pay grade when someone put Brennan Manning's *The Ragamuffin Gospel* into my hands.

I'd known God's stories, God's creative power, and God's instructions. I'd known God's people, and the buildings they'd built, and the rhythms in which they'd run them. I'd memorized God's people's beliefs. I had comprehended on some level what it meant for me to love God's Son. But I don't think, until this book, that I ever knew God's love.

Brennan Manning's writing made me feel sacredly human. It made me feel all right about being human. It made me feel connected (on some level) to the rest of humanity, for which he emphasized Jesus cared so much, in a way I had not yet experienced. We were all in need of a little more than we were saying. We were all being offered a little more than we were realizing by a God who was loving us a little more than we were comprehending.

"For God so loved the world . . . " it said in John 3:16.

The words, as I revisited while reading Manning's book, went from the fast recitation of my youth to a slow dissection of significance and depth.

For God.

God.

So loved.

So . . . loved.

The world.

For God *so* loved *this* world.

I'd spent so much time fighting against the idea of grace as the dangerous and diluting turpentine of truth that I thought it was. But grace was something altogether different, I was beginning to discover. It was not synonymous with liberalism, tolerance, acceptance, and enabling compassion. It did not need to be qualified by my definition of truth in order for it to be the very essence of God.

Grace was being known by God, and radically, unconditionally loved and invited anyway. Everybody.

It was being met and seen by God like I was being met and seen by those friends whose upturned hands were receiving my confessions; like I was being met and seen by the folks who were trying to make connections with me despite my insistence on changing them. Grace was a gift I could never merit and that could never be taken away.

The cup called "Righteousness" that lived inside of my chest, right next to teleported Jesus and his TV dinner, had been one that I'd spent the last set of years working so very hard as the priest and now the Levite to fill up and pour out, fill up and pour out, one way or another. But grace, for this ragamuffin, became the thing that told that cup to stay put and breathe deeply. Grace is what began filling it right on up until it poured past the brim and kept on pouring, no muscle of my own needed.

It felt as if a job description that I had written for myself long ago had been taken out of my hands and edited. And I was eased.

But what then, if not behavior-management? What then, if not clean hands and a pure heart? What then, if not baiting unbelievers with listening ears so that we may gain an audience to tell them about the free and full ways of Christ? *What then must I do, Lord*—the seeker in me cried out again—if not spend all of my energy making sure that those I love are thinking and choosing correctly?

Lines Drawn

Amidst all of the sloughing off of self-imposed rules and regulated religion, I accompanied my family to meet my granddad's mistress for the first and last time. Her hair was wild like a cockatoo and her arms enclosed by the tight leopard print of a pre-teen's weekend shopping. She hugged my dad tightly as she explained how much she had heard about him over the years, as if they were distant cousins, as if they were not forever the enemies of each other's past ideals.

Her forty-something-year-old daughter winced nervously, like we all did, as her mom hung on the edge of our van window and raved on about her time with a man that I'll never know; that my dad barely knew. She pushed a book title onto us and asked that we please read her memoir about all the backstory for which my dad had only ever seen symptoms. The brothels, the mob, the drugs, the fraud, the shady life that led to a violent death; the life that led to three families, grown simultaneously, laying eyes on each other for the first time over a casket guarded by a perimeter of sunglass-shaded men in black.

I thought about my grandmother back home—kind, goofy, nervous. I thought about the stories that my dad would tell of how his dad would drop in periodically and unpredictably during those first sixteen years of his life to share his charm and his gifts, but never child support. I thought about the stories he would tell anytime my brother and I would dare complain about wanting more stuff or of being so bored, stories of not having two dollars to see a baseball game and therefore watching from a parking lot tree. He would tell stories of having to be raised by a handful of stand-up guys from our town who stepped in when Charles went to jail; stories of getting to go to college only on the back of the social security money that came after the third woman shot him. College: an experience that came at such a cost for him and an experience that I had mostly whined about thus far because of "sinners" and the preachers who excused them.

All of the stories bubbled around my head while the mistress spoke, and I watched my dad connect dots that seemed so unfair for him to have to be connecting. I wondered how the most emotionally sound, generous, and available man I knew could come from one background and be equipped in heart and spirit to offer an entirely different experience to his family. My dad: the cycle-breaker and way-maker.

To know that this person whom I loved had experienced something so emotionally painful was too emotionally painful for me to wrap my mind around. Having and receiving had often been a mixed bag throughout my childhood because of pieces of his reality that echoed throughout mine. I could not accept gifts without a decent amount of inner turmoil. Perpetually aware that good people sometimes suffer and that I had lived with one who had, it was hard to ignore that the scales were off.

Eventually, we went home and never really spoke of Charles's life or women much again.

And then, one Thursday night back at school, the chaplain of the college stretched a line of duct tape across the room, spanning between two signs that read "agree" and "disagree." I fumed in the corner wondering what was the point of an exercise so divisive? "Weren't we to be creating unity?" I seethed, unaware of my deep fear of being discovered as a person without answers—like the lukewarm lenients standing at the line's muddled middle.

"I'm going to say a phrase or a sentence, and then all of you will choose your spots along the spectrum," she announced. "We will have explanations offered by each stance. The first one is: Homosexuality is Wrong . . ."

I took to my wall with the nostril-fumes of a raging bull. Across the room, connected in their common convictions next to the sign reading "disagree," stood my classmates—my peers from study groups, and weekly worship, and the cafeteria—feeling judged by me feeling judged by them. My Levite reality was breaking down in a moment when I could no longer be stealthy about my sinner-love/sin-hate.

There was no room in that room, in that activity, for my friendships to be a means to an end. There was only room for *an end*. There was only room for me to take to a side that I thought to be most faithful, to look again like the priest that I had been working so hard not to be; only room for me to break the ties between the relationships that I had made, stare at the carpet and, *out of* faithfulness and reluctance, agree.

"Unrelational, waste of time, toxic!" I ranted about it for years. I wanted no part in whatever *that* activity or the logic that had created it was. I wanted no part in a religion that was so busy figuring out what side of the room they were going to stand on while children like my dad lived in a world of instability and lack. I wanted no part in missing the opportunities to make things better for them all because I was too distracted by stance-ensuring. I felt burdened by the small notion of inequality I had witnessed in my family, burdened by the lack of fruit I was seeing in myself in all the drama that was being the story's Levite. I felt burdened and ready to redirect whenever the next worldview would kindly open itself up for me.

Slowly, I began to adjust to the weight of it all by resolving that the only way to break out of the legalism while stomaching my privilege was to live in a way that others too could have what they needed. And this was more important—*had to be* more important—than going around clarifying what one thought about people's decisions all the time.

I began to listen to preachers introduce the notion of "world changers." I began to take note of how that often connected to Third World countries or the rougher parts of a city. Fixing people's habits regarding sexuality, beer, and doubts while loving God and loving them had become too great of a burden to bear and one from which I'd felt God's real grace had at least partially freed me. But maybe fixing people's circumstances—providing for their basic needs and *then* their spiritual needs—would turn out to be more doable.

Maybe it would feel more alive. Maybe it would feel more like Jesus finally stepping out of that rainy stained glass window and into the actual world where water is given to the thirsty and little boys with big hearts don't have to watch baseball games from tree branches. Maybe my faith could become more practical, action oriented, and transcendent of the arguments with something that couldn't be argued with: pure, radical service.

Maybe this service was greater than judgement. Maybe the unfamiliar mission field would feel more alive than a preacher's microphone. Maybe it would finally be the biggest, best, and most. Maybe this was the way of those who loved God enough to let it change them, who were changed enough to be able to change the reality around them.

At the end of my freshman year, on the hopes that these thoughts were even remotely true, I ditched the world of belief-clarification and duct-tape-divided rugs and hopped my first plane to Washington, D.C. I moved into the barred Sunday school annex of an American Baptist church out of which I'd be leading groups of high schoolers into "serving the poor" for the summer; out of which, my world would shift entirely, for better or worse.

4

Irresistible

The Samaritan

Out of breath, you rake your hands under his shoulders, shoveling dirt into your fingernails in a manner that makes the hairs on your neck bristle. You fold your bad left knee under your outstretched right and heave his torso up into your lap. You'd be crying if your adrenaline wasn't pumping so. How . . . could anyone do this to anyone?

He's breathing, oh God, good he's breathing. And there's a pulse drumming in his jowls, surging blood to the swollen battlefields of his body. You overextend your arm behind you to reach the bag in which you keep the extra supplies. This isn't your first rodeo—not on this road, not in these parts. As you pour the wine and oil into the cuts, wiping, and wrapping, and waiting for the yelps of anguish to subside, you briefly think about the folks back home who have names and made-up-minds about people like him— just like you once did.

Briefly. You think about this briefly, because you stopped listening to that nonsense when you began to notice that people like him were being picked off of this very highway and tossed out of the line of sight and aid like pieces of trash.

People like him, with hands, feet, and family, aren't altogether different from your own hands, feet, and family, you've come to realize.

There is risk, to be sure: religious risks, safety risks, convenience risks. But those nervous calculations and unreasonable rituals have kept far too many people rotting on roadsides for longer than you can think about, and you've decided that not another single human will do so on your watch.

His dehydrated everything is not entirely convincing that he'll have enough life to stretch the night. Hurling his weight onto your personal transportation, the two of you set out to find a place where he might land for a while. You, drenched and disgusting, keep thinking about the story that this will one day be.

One day, when his wounds are thick scars and his life is back in order. One day, when this very moment inspires him to leave behind the lesser life that got him here. One day, when your people groups are nicer to each other because of how you took the time and the care. One day, when even the robbers will come around and start bandaging instead of beating.

One day, when the effort is rewarded with the full redemption for which you are risking a whole hell of a lot. That will be a good day, one day. That will be a worthwhile tale.

New Eyes

STEPPING OUT OF THE team van onto the asphalt of the church parking lot on the corner of 10th and R, I felt brave, and obedient, and ready for my God and neighbor love to manifest itself in a way that mattered the most that I thought it had ever mattered; in a way that superseded arguments stoked, and lines drawn, and obsessive clarification prioritized.

I felt intrinsically sent and immediately out of place.

As the only Southerner on a team of people from Pennsylvania, Missouri, and New Jersey, I was jarred by the disappointment of my team dynamic. I had left disagreement to find faithfulness only to land in another pile of disagreement once again. It was evident from the moment I arrived that my first and greatest obstacle would be John.

My teammate John was a tall, extroverted Democrat who I could have hurled out of a window during our first conversation. His liberal ideologies seemed as watertight as his voice was loud, and I felt frequently suspicious that every conversation we were having was meant to destroy the very moral platform on which my beliefs and practices rested. John would spar with our other more willing coworkers about theology, policy, and topics of sexuality and faith. I'd cry myself to sleep wishing we could just keep binary topics off the discussion table and dedicate ourselves to not letting the devil distract us from *keeping the main thing the main thing.* He'd talk about race relations and recycling; I'd note them as code words for content in which I thought the church had no business meddling.

In addition to fighting the powers and principalities of political time-wasters I had moved to escape, the reality of how far I was from home and the feeling of being severely under-qualified for my summer job were ever present mind-wars. Up to this point, I had witnessed very minor destitution, only counting the Christmas trips with my home church to drop off food baskets to embarrassed classmates or the occasional summer painting of widow's houses. Those childhood moments were uncomfortable, but D.C. was silencing.

Living and working in Washington was an overwhelming enigma from the beginning. Four blocks from the concrete jungle of bills and laws, I would stir pasta salad for a hundred hungry vets, angsty teens who were there to "love on people," and wealthy, black church members who seemed to have mixed emotions about us being there. The barred annex had been the home of this eighteen-year-old and my griping coworkers for barely three weeks, and I felt three times as outnumbered, disoriented, and young as I did when I first moved to college. Reality could not keep up with my romanticism; it has always struggled to do so.

My eyelids retreated back into my headache-occupied face, batting hard for the morning's focus. A slightly deflated air mattress, the buzz of people taking turns brushing their teeth in shower-less bathrooms below, the honks and breaks of an antsy neighborhood getting an early start to its day, were noisy unfamiliarities for my senses. This was my new home for eleven long weeks.

The adventure that had been so exhilarating to anticipate had now become work: hard work. Our sites (like the nation's largest homeless shelter, a cerebral palsy care facility, a food distributor for AIDS patients) were emotionally draining like longsuffering service that would continue chugging along years after we were no longer residents of the Northwest Quadrant. The nights were heavy too, full of group discussions and weighted, passionate sentiments of high-schoolers and their dedicated adults.

I was learning the loaded life of the Samaritan—what it meant to actually *care* to stop on the road. I could lead a worship service and stir up a pretty good discussion; I could defend my thoughts on sin every time John would bring up specifics on our walks to get pizza. But care for the hurting did not, in any world, come naturally. It was not that I didn't have a heart for the wounded; it was as if I could not even see them.

I had been casting my pennies in the Levite's pond so determinedly that all my eyes were set to notice were a few moral decisions of middle-class white folks. The true north of my compass was all about how one might connect personally to God. And D.C. was revealing to me that there were people here too and that there might be such a thing as corporate sin and corporate grace.

Let me say that again: it's as if D.C. showed me for the first time that there were people here too, and that they were important to the life of my faith.

"I need new eyes," I'd pray as I'd find myself glancing over my shoulder at John in hopes of getting an education on how to love someone who was in need. He was so good at it, despite his theology.

One weekend, I migrated to my fourth Sunday school classroom in the annex after hours of tapping desks and struggling without success to make my nighttime messages less boring and more motivational like the good preachers and pray-ers. My teammates had gone to Mass while I lingered behind, too young to drive the vans, too skeptical of Catholicism to join, and exactly thirty minutes of stir-crazy away from eating my own fist or piercing both eyeballs with the pointed ends of Sharpies. I was a prisoner in my calling, wearily searching for sermon material that pertained to this new environment and too leery of the book suggestions that my D.C. teammates had been pushing as prompts for my messages. I decided to take a walk and get a little air.

I grabbed my key and my phone and headed down 10th street with a bebopping invincibility. With a do-gooder-for-God-meets-world outlook and a deep desire to find anything familiar, I went exploring alone, and eighteen, and hours of flights away from family, and hours of Mass away from peers. *But God protects those who do God's will*, I'd deduced from the stewardship sermons and all the freak stories about faithful people being spared from tragedy. I was untouchable.

A sandwich sign popped out of the consumer scene, and I ran like a child. I knew this chain. We had these sandwiches back home. These sandwiches were as close to Louisiana as I had found. I ducked in and ordered a chocolate chip cookie and a large Diet Coke in the first styrofoam cup that I'd been able to buy since joining the company of John-the-Recycler. John-the-Aspartame-Snob. Fueled on caffeine and high on more vitamin D than I'd had in a week, I continued my meandering around the local shops.

"Hey girl, yeah you. Can you spare some cash for a hungry man?" His bloodshot eyes served as the warning signs I was happy to ignore. *Give to anyone who has need*, the Bible had said; and I was trying to now take it seriously. *He is the wounded; I am the Samaritan. This is what Samaritans do.* I reached into my backpack and thumbed out a ten.

"Here you go, sir, but look I've prayed over this money. So I'm trusting that you'll put it to good use and to God's glory," a cracking voice served as the polygraph spike that indicated I'd not done much of this kind of thing before.

"You said 'sir,'" he reached for the money, grabbing ahold of my fingers on the bill's other side. "You must not be from around here."

"I'm from around here," I said, searching for competency . . . confidence . . . bigness.

"Well, Miss From-Around-Here, you have something on your face." One hand never left the money or my fingers, the other raised itself to my cheek. My heart began racing as I watched his head turn to look down the alley just fifteen feet behind us with his hands so close to me. On the verge of screaming, I snatched my arms away and called back for him to have a blessed day as I ran as fast as I'd ever run to the nearest Rite Aid where I cried in the funny card aisle until I could get up the nerve to make it all the way back home to the annex.

I was there for hours: sobbing, and checking the window, and wondering how a woman was ever to be the Good Samaritan like a man could be the Good Samaritan in this world.

When I rounded the corner to the church's soccer field, rattled and traumatized by the feeling of *what if*, Vickie was sitting unavoidably on a bench between me and the door I'd been so desperate to reenter. *I don't have it in me for another poor person today*, I gulped.

But either her maternal aura or her quick disclaimer disarmed me before I could ignore her like the Levite I was used to being— that I had felt so justified in being just moments before.

"Don't mind me, child. I just come back here sometimes to look at the hoops. My son and I would play ball in this park when he was a boy. He's got his own place now, and I couldn't be more proud," she said, her brown-bagged bottle resting in the gravel.

I let myself pause—like a proper, people-acknowledging, peace-filled Samaritan pause. We talked about the summer ahead of me; she asked for nothing except to maybe visit on days that weren't too hot, swearing to come sober next time. I felt a bit of rewiring happening within me as I saw someone "like her" for possibly the first time ever: someone poor and not altogether "other" like I had previously categorized.

I felt a bit of rewiring as I, tilting my head in curiosity like a dog, observed someone who deserved to live a life not so bound to bottles and benches as beds, someone not threatening like the alley-man had felt threatening, someone that I could wrap my mind around loving to wholeness regardless of where she stood in her beliefs or having to know them beforehand. She looked like someone that I could spend my one precious life saving.

And though we said goodbye forever that day, she was a spirit who had blown in long enough to ignite a pilot light within me. I ran the last twenty feet into the annex, shoving the door closed and locked behind me, rushing through the building making certain that every closet and every bathroom was empty of monstrous men. I was home, and safe, and my mother could never know that I'd gone wandering in D.C. by myself that day. She could never know that the veil of my invincibility had been ripped right down its center, or that I was somehow newly awakened to and fearful of a beautiful and broken world from which I could now no longer be shielded and from which I maybe no longer wished to be.

As I plopped down at one of the skinny, rectangle tables in the common space and pulled out my letters from back home just to hold them, I noticed that resting nearby, heckling me like a great-uncle at a family reunion, was one of John's books that he'd all but bribed me to open for my sermon-writing. I liked its shape, liked its smell, and liked its title. I was pre-annoyed by its content because of all that John stood for, but things were shifting, and everyone was still at Mass and not hovering closely enough to incite my stubbornness with their enthusiasm. Additionally, I was just grateful to be alive and feeling willing.

So, all things considered, I began reading Shane Claiborne's *The Irresistible Revolution*, and I stayed up all night reading. I stayed up all through that long night changing my mind, soaking the words up like water for my readied and thirsty faith.

Shane's understanding of a love revolution for Jesus (and what that meant for the roadside-wounded and new Samaritans such as myself) sounded alive, close, doable, and important. His book was, in that very vulnerable moment, giving language to a life I didn't know I'd been needing to live. It was *good news*—actual news that sounded good—and I felt like I was finally starting to know what that meant. Shane's book was putting words and examples to an existence of shared possessions, radical generosity, leveraged privilege, and a God whose words were more than just vapid suggestions. It sounded like the most adventurous and purposeful life *could* actually be a life for God. It sure sounded like love that had learned how to walk around. And I needed that; I needed to be that.

Immediately, I wanted the exact life that Shane had written about. It was the only one that I now knew of that sounded so freeing and purposeful. Greater than rules kept and lines drawn, sinners loved but sin still checked, it was an invitation to be a part of the real world with a real faith like Jesus had been and had. I wanted to conduct sit-ins for homeless people, sleep on the ground, watch food be multiplied because I worked for God on behalf of the poor. I wanted to give away my extra coats, and make sure my food didn't exploit child-slaves, and live in a home with lots of people who weren't necessarily family. I wanted to grow gardens in abandoned lots, shape old weapons into tools, and play with neighbors, cops, refugees, and prostitutes in fire hydrant water on a street that I called my block.

When I closed the back cover of that little brown book and stared out the barred window of the annex, I felt as if that Sunday morning faith that I had so hoped would spill out of stained glass windows and into my honest to God, whole life was finally doing just that. I am crying just thinking about it now, despite the years of complexities and pain that were ahead. Jesus wanted something from me, and it went far past my boring memorization of Scripture and how close I was willing to get to my hedonistic classmates before retracting.

He wanted to step outside of the boxes I had created for politics and denominations; he wanted the way I spent my money, and shared my kitchen, and answered my front door, and talked about skin color to reflect the fact that his kingdom was in all and for all. John said that Shane Claiborne invited him into his own faith, and

I agreed as he squealed over the fact that I had started, and finished, and (gasp) been so impacted by a book suggested by someone who voted as blue as he. But it was true. Shane's book invited me into my faith that night (or at least the version of my faith that could plug into the real world). And that shifted the course of so much.

My friendship with John began to peek its head through our differences after that. We'd volunteer to do the Sunday laundry together each week, loading up the washers with quarters and walking down to the nearest McDonald's where he'd buy me a Diet Coke and I'd ask him to teach me what it meant to shop fair trade. We'd gush about our favorite campers from the week before and share our thoughts about God with a bit more care for each other.

I taught him how to say "y'all" and explained the importance of garlic salt in taco meat and why I thought we were still supposed to challenge personal morality but also now serve the poor. He'd explain to me why it's crucial that we care for creation, make good art, and love peace. Then, we'd scream the hook from the Killers' "All These Things that I've Done" as we'd drive back home to prepare for another week of long hours, heavy stories, and character-shifting within the parable that was turning out to be my life.

Ruby

When I returned from D.C. that fall for my second year of college, born again (again, again) into a faith that was now alive and active in the world, I stumbled back into Shreveport like a war vet. My stubborn refusal to use money and my new obsession with wearing head wraps quickly concerned my friends and family almost more than did the fact that my "y'alls" had been entirely replaced with "you guys."

"But I taught them to season their taco meat!" I'd justify, as if that were a solid Southern compensation for throwing a fit about my family's Disney World trip that was being planned when "people were going hungry, for the love of God." I changed my major because "life is short," and I began to push Shane's book as the liberating game-changer that I knew it would be. Our local

Lifeway began carrying it on their shelf after my tenth at-the-counter order, and I felt a new sort of revival coming.

Being in school for three additional years at a private liberal arts college, with our pizza bar and landscaped gardens, was a difficult reality to reconcile within my changing heart. I had made Shane's community, The Simple Way (and all their actions and efforts that I had read about) my ultimate objective and my newest definition of right living. All other efforts, all other lifestyles—including and especially my own of expensive education—felt as if they only fell short.

The life of a Good Samaritan, no longer blinded in sight or corroded in heart to the poor and the bleeding, was now the definition of *the way*. It *was* full life. It *was* purpose. It *was* the answer that Jesus gave to that poor seeker in me who took the long way through priesthood and Levitism to understand it. To save the lost had been obedient, but to save the poor was now heroic and necessary because *who cared to hear about hell after death if hell was their reality now?* I'd been called to be a rescuer, and I could not fathom numbing out to my convictions until graduation. On Thursday nights in our low-lit chapel, I'd prompt our confession group: what more can we do *right now* for the poor?

Through a series of trial-and-error attempts at meeting people who lived under the poverty line—like taking hot chocolate to the bus station or playing bingo at the soup kitchen that one time—I was finally able to make my only real friendship with the first homeless person whose name I actually knew since Vickie.

We found Ruby drenched in rain water at an intersection one Saturday and bought her a tent for the property on which she lived until Carl (the home-owner: a kooky, once-homeless cab driver) got arrested for storing so very many Chihuahuas in his freezer just feet beyond where we'd sit with her on Friday nights.

Ruby had a beautiful Native American bone structure and leathery, curled fingers riddled with arthritis. They'd look like tree roots when she'd use their odd contortions to open water bottles and light cigarettes. She had a skepticism toward doctors and a problem with cocaine—an addiction I discovered once after finding her crack pipe in some soured clothes I'd volunteered to wash. She'd have no time to dismiss her customers or dealers before we'd show up without warning to force her into a game of Catchphrase that would make her old eyes crinkle with laughter.

She was kind and complimentary, for the most part pleasant company. Her path for restoration was easy to identify, I thought; it was logical even. Get fed, get clothed, get clean, get a job, get a home, get your kids back, thank Jesus. I was ready to walk with her so long as the dots connected forwardly. Ruby would brush her long hair and water the plants that she said reminded her of being alive, and we'd take her chicken strips and play the newest songs that our worship band had written while pressing her to go in for a check-up. One day, she saved up enough money from her social security checks to buy a shed on whose door she pinned a piece of notebook paper that read, "Jesus Christ is the Ruler of this House." And we all celebrated.

But it was hard not to quickly and completely fix Ruby. It was hard not to see miracles in the way that I'd anticipated them. It was hard not to have the closing date of a summer internship waiting on me at the end of serving her. It was hard not to have her complete and total compliance and gratitude when it came to getting her bandaged, fed, and provided for like the Samaritan had done in his seemingly smooth gesture towards goodness. It was frustrating not to understand her world and the things she did to survive.

I would picture her clean, healed, and working. I would picture her free of piss smell and the men that made their deals with her aching body. I needed her to show me that this life I was hoping to come fully into after graduation would be one where people do good and other people get better. But she couldn't.

I don't know when we stopped going or answering. I assume it was when the lies became too heavy and I concluded that I was not yet emotionally resourced enough to know where to go next in our friendship. For the last year of college (and many of the years since), I avoided looking down the five hundred block of Egan Street, worried I'd catch her eye as she brushed her gray locks on

Carl's old porch, forcing me to admit I'd given up on her. Her: my only outlet for a radical life.

Every now and then, still a decade later, Ruby will come across a new phone with a tiny bit of data on it and send one of us a text to say how much she loves us. And her grace became the miracle in my willingness to ditch her complicated story and find a group of roadside-wounded folks who would line up better with the narrative that I felt I needed.

Ruby represented a gritty system and a threat to my dualistic worldview that I was not yet ready to question. So I retreated and waited for direction on how I might find a cleaner, clearer Samaritan story for myself, where we all live right and the world heals because of it.

In the meantime, I would dabble in all the missional ways that I knew how as an undergrad. I began tutoring in an under-resourced neighborhood where I was interviewed and photographed on my first day there for the organization's brochure. My peach skin in a sea of brown was plastered on its marketing for a decade; and all the while, I knew that it was never *not* a chore to show up in that place that made me feel rich, and naive, and also a little bored.

I sold T-shirts to my college campus after hearing about a famine in Africa; I secured a spot on a summer team to Kenya where I did little more than take gorgeous pictures, be stunned by the abundance of poverty, and piddle in expensive busywork for fourteen days. I spoke at women's groups on the weekends where I'd wear my Kenyan skirts and my continent of Africa necklace and accuse them of not doing better for the world, charging them with radical living that was available for them to have as adults like it was not yet available for me to have while bound to the timeline of my diploma.

"I just want to remind everyone about all the things that our group actually does for missions," the leader would say in an effort to smooth over my awkwardly concluded commission. "Britney is learning some wonderful things in her college years, isn't she?"

"Excuses," I'd lament as I'd gather up my soapstone elephants. "I hope I am never kept from a faithful life by my excuses; by tagging them to the young passions of a twenty-year-old idealist. Just wait until I am fully free," I'd think. I was so anxious to be.

"I will prove to you all that these are not just the whims of a college student. I will prove to myself that I can and will live a life of risky, radical yeses no matter what season I am in, for the rest of my days."

Shared Sandwiches

In 2009, I was twenty-one, gliding on the newness of having just graduated and being released to embrace all parts of full life to which God had been alluring me. Living in an apartment with two girlfriends, I was working three hours a day for the richest church in town, leading their teams to the southern part of Hispaniola. It was such good and risky work that from the beginning, and for a while, I felt very little else was required of my life. We were feeding and clothing, healing and building in whirlwind blitzes every month and a half. In between trips, I would tan by our fancy pool, sip lattes while hoping to find a single "world-changing" man to date, and not meet my neighbors.

Haiti was the place of my biggest, best, and fullest dreams. It was an adventure every single time we'd visit. While in country, the languages, shifting back and forth in their translations, swirled around my ears as if designed by an indie filmmaker. The fabrics—hand patched and handwashed—made me want more of everything foreign. Our afternoons of turning flips in the clear coastal waters of Ile a Vache and the nights of playing Uno with our translators and missing each other's cultural wits, all collected into a lush archive of stories for my life.

The feeling of sun-drawn lines on shoulders, the smell of gasoline, sweat, and coconut trees. The colors of pastel houses standing in stark contrast to all that red, sticky clay. The babies with their songs and without their parents who invited us into their lives to learn dances and build wells . . . it was all something so substantial to write home about.

It was substantial, and brave, and good, and unable to really be fact-checked by followers who were drawn in by the distance of it all. What magic.

The "mission field" was saturated with a story that I didn't want to be left out of, and here I was living into it in the most convenient way possible. Here I was, mildly pressing into the life about which Shane had written, definitely pressing into the life that had been exampled by the Samaritan who stopped to bandage and better the poor just as I was now doing every six weeks.

In Les Cayes—in the south of Haiti—the Scriptures about primitive parts of life (water wells, livestock, crops, and boats) seemed to peel right out of the Bible's pages. The fatherless and widowed shared home, responsibility, and family. It was less easy to get distracted by material possessions, social media updates, mindless matters like theological arguments and politics. Haiti made me feel energized, close to God, to the soil, to people, and to purpose.

Papa's House was an orphan village (nearly impossible to get to during hurricane season) that housed eighty baby bodies with their distended bellies and scaly scalps. To get there, our team would hold tightly to the rails welded around the back end of a small Toyota. The motos and tap taps dripping with people in work clothes and rags zipped around us, the stoic faces unruffled by our daring travels and pale skin.

The smells of burning trash, baking bread, and blooming banana trees created a continuum of ever-changing odor as the piles of coconuts and the periodic snack shacks would blur on by. Our truck would stop often—when stuck in mud, when out of gas, when a passenger needed to trot off into the woods to take a squat. What may have taken fifteen minutes with solid highway infrastructure, consistently took us an hour each way. Once we'd arrive, a hundred bony hands would swarm our hips in a grand welcome of the Americans. The first chunk of each day was spent with everyone holding each other, which is something that seems far more valuable now than it did then.

Evens was a quiet five-year-old whose hand would sneak into mine as we sorted the stuffed animals and Flintstone vitamins that we'd been so glad to get past customs. I thought he looked like an infant though his friends would cackle from the bushes about his new, white girlfriend. I'd pull him onto the scale, clipboard in hand, and write down his weight of twenty-five pounds. Our goal was to return frequently and for his body mass to have increased each time.

We'd come to spend a little over two weeks in country, laying groundwork for an orphan sponsor program, putting on a couple of vacation Bible schools and soccer camps, delivering supplies, paying for belly-worm treatments, and taking inventory of all that needed to be fixed or provided in the ways that we could fix and provide them. There was little chance of not feeling accomplished or irrefutably helpful in such a fast and fruitful whirlwind.

It was our first day on site when we noticed that no one on the property was making any movement toward stopping for lunch. Ignorant of the village's common practice of only eating two big meals a day, we teared up in the corners of dusty classrooms as we collectively decided to forego eating as well. Instead, we would combine our sandwiches, chips, and cookies into a large stash to be divided among the tens and tens of children.

Lining them up for the salvation of a few bites, we made the mistake of putting one of the group's only parents in charge of distribution—her throbbing mama heart unable to skimp and our nerves escalating as we watched kids scamper off happily with uneconomic fistfuls. We'd wince at each other over the tops of their heads, then to the diminishing food pile, then to the line's length.

But the food never stopped, and the sandwiches just kept breaking. I don't know what to say to this now, other than regardless of how skeptical I have become of my own romantic, rose-colored glasses worn during those days, regardless of how naively we may have approached the moment (. . . the mission . . . the culture), the food still stretched. In a way that it shouldn't have.

Wi!

Trip leading in Haiti soon became second nature. The forms to fill out before stepping onto the tarmac, the island band awaiting us at the bottom of the terminal escalator, the Kreyol (Creole) learned and lost and learned again, the team packing-prep and malaria meds reminders, the emails with their *Bonjou* greetings, the books read and devotions written about foreign poverty ministry, the growing ease of travel wisdom wedged between gullibility and self-preservation, the early morning airport drop-offs, the way I'd learned to sleep on that five-hour God-forsakenly bumpy ride to the southern coast, the miracle of how much would change for those we were helping between trips: it all became a part of a normal, adventurous, and *good* life for three years.

The children were gaining weight, and school desks, and some extra privacy. Clean water systems had been installed, and Haitians had been trained to run them. Outdoor pavilions, playgrounds, and rabbit cages were constructed with funds that 200 stateside sponsors had been recruited to donate. A second village had been added to our partnerships, and round two of problem and provision inventory-taking had begun.

This was the pace and content for which I'd felt made.

I would travel with my laptop and write lengthy blog posts about how we'd seen food multiplied and children learning math, how we'd been able to drink the water out of the system we had built at the complex, how we'd given the Haitians a chance to teach us things like their national anthem and Rara dance. I'd share how Evens was gaining weight and a little bit of a personality, and I'd prove it with staggering stats and beautifully bright pictures. I'd write about how I threw up the one time I was brave enough to eat goat from a street stand. I'd write about the feet of the orphanage "mamas" that we'd offered to wash.

And readers back home would see things like:

> *Three buckets of clean water from the new clean water building were heaved onto the floor, sloshing parasite-free goodness all about. We unzipped supply bags and layered*

dresses on display, stacked nail polishes of reds and pinks, and grew suds in pails with fast moving, gloved hands.

The women began to line up in the room where our translator helped us explain: "We wanted to have a celebration just for you. Because we realize that we get to visit for a week or two, enjoy the children and our time here, but then leave. And we recognize that the real work comes from you. Our lives have been changed by these villages and these children, and we know that they are only here because of the meals that you cook, the clothes that you wash, the beds that you make, and the wounds that you bandage. And we wanted to say thank you. So if you will let us, we would love to wash your feet and hands, paint your nails, do your makeup, and let you choose some dresses and purses that we've brought."

We waited a bit nervously wondering if they would be offended by our offer, when a huge unanimous "Wi!" came from each animated face around the room.

A small wave of uneasiness quickly followed our eagerness when we realized that the hands and feet we would be pampering had been caked with experience and malady. But the fear of the unfamiliar in the form of gnarled toes, missing nails, heel infections, or encrusted mud quickly dissolved because, well, there was now no turning back.

The long morning felt like hard work and also worship, a nod toward each other as we silently and collectively considered that each woman might be Jesus. As if every knot we pressed into, stain we scrubbed, muscle we relaxed could be his own. As if each tension spot massaged were a thank you for a child being picked up, a plate being washed, a tummy being medicated. As if we were getting the opportunity to tangibly thank God for individually caring for those orphans whom we loved.

Each mama came through the different stations picking the colors and lotions they wanted and sharing with us shy, loving glances as they watched each other and rested. Toward the end, the mama of the mamas, as she was revered, with her perpetual frown that climbed to the top of her string-bean body, gave a speech.

"What you have given us is worth more than gold or silver. We know you do this because of the love in your

heart. And because you have loved us, we can love the chil-
dren better." Her scowl never shifting, she grabbed four of
us by the necks and sobbed into our shoulders.

I'd write about how everything seemed to be growing and everything seemed to be alive; how we would continue to say yes to God and to our role as good Samaritans so long as there were bellies in those buildings that needed feeding and so long as there was always a rooftop on which our teams could gather to debrief a solid day of eating, serving, and dreaming together.

But I wouldn't write about how hard it was to keep up with where all the money was being used, how unnerving and unpredictable the riots caused by governmental instabilities were becoming, how not all of our partnerships seemed to be disclosing all of the important information needed for the operations we were trying to run 1,500 miles away. I wouldn't write about how I felt progressively like I was living two lives—one of beans and rice and service and one of pools, and lattes, and hiding from chatty Mrs. Mavis who lived next door. I would not write about how burnt out I was becoming back home as a missions director for a megachurch—the poor people's pastor in a world of wealth. I wouldn't write about my growing concerns about systemic injustice that felt beyond me and our efforts or my growing doubts about a God who would allow them in the first place.

I wouldn't write about my questions, because I'd found who Jesus needed me—and all of us—to be. And questioning that may mean that the suffering I'd been too distracted by "fixing" to fully see was indeed closer than I was comfortable with admitting. It might mean I'd have to reenter a rat-race of crafting, searching, and redefining once again, while I just really wanted to have arrived (as one would assume they had arrived once they'd lived the life of the Samaritan: the story's hero).

But disregarding an increasingly rushing current within me, blinding myself with even more efforts and even more trips and projects, would only make for a more shocking and traumatic waterfall of upheaval ahead. In my passionate promotion of the positives and the miracles *only*—in my still incessant need to have the answers, avoid hopelessness, and defend a sometimes confusing God and his world—I left me such little room to be wrong. And this would leave me so few options but to cut, run, and redirect when things began to look like they might crumble within and around me.

5

Raging Blame

The Robbers as Them

His blood is clotting to paste, and the swollen tissue is closing up tightly around his cuts as your animal hauls him off to his best chance. The reality of the body rushing its white cells to wounds, plumping up the lacerations with a generously focused healing, makes you feel like you are on the right side of wrongdoing.

You had no idea there would turn out to be so much complicated evil (or at least, fragility) amongst the good in this dark and beautiful world.

How could they?

How could God?

How could anyone?

What makes for a world so sick?

Off in the distance, you hear them, or it, or something (or so you think you do) carrying on with their voices and choices so unlike your own. With their secrets, and the things to which they expose their children, and their poor conflict-resolution skills, and their willingness to dehumanize, and the way that they mimic this unpredictably disastrous land, and their god who asks them to do

wretched things with their loyalty, and their interpreta-
tions of Scripture, and the ways they are stingy with their
love and greedy with their money and disconnected with
their votes. The way that they squeeze the goodness out of
the ground leaving it riddled with carcinogenic cruelty and
the way the ground absorbs the ones we thought would be
here longer. The ways they repeat history and abuse cycles.
The way they are hurtful with their hurt.

Off in the distance, you hear the uncontrollable
storms, and those faceless people, and their atrocious sys-
tems, and (somewhere among them) the Creator who gave
them the room to do all that they do.

And it makes you so anxious. And it makes you so
skeptical of the good, and the bad, and your ability to dis-
cern either.

Cancer

"WHY DON'T WE JUST send them birth control?" a woman from
the back of the Sunday school class to whom I'd been asked to
speak between trips said, as she bobbed her high-heel and tapped
her pencil.

"Well, Haiti is a predominantly Catholic country so . . ."

"I thought they were all practitioners of Voodoo, sticking
pins in dolls and stuff while they feed their children mud biscuits.
That's what I read online," another class member interrupted me.

"Actually, if you read into the backstory of Voodoo, much
of it comes from Haitian slave history where their ancestors were
unable to carry over the traditions of their African religions and
therefore had to hide their rituals within the practices of a forced
and oppressive Christianity, and *speaking of* slave history . . . Did
you know that Haiti was the first Western society to gain indepen-
dence from slavery and establish a free black republic? It's actually
very interesting (and truly horrible) how the United States refused
to recognize Haiti as a free and independent country during the
years before its own emancipation . . ."

"Ok, but why can't they grow their own food? Why do we have to send it?"

I'd begun stress-sweating with every sentence they would not allow me to finish.

"Well," I took a breath, "we don't send all of it, just some of it. And some of it we help to grow by . . ."

"So aren't you putting some farmers out of work by sending food? Couldn't that be adding back into the cycle by harming the economy, by ending jobs of those who then can't feed their children, who *then* have to become economic orphans? Are any of the children we sponsor economic orphans?"

"Well, I hadn't really thought . . .," I stumbled, blindsided by the chance that she who was so unwilling to learn might be teaching me—who was so unwilling to learn—something.

"I'm not sure I want to give to this effort," her bobbing foot shaking her whole body as she said it. "But we appreciate you coming by. It's a lot to think about," she concluded as I stacked my brochures and waved a withered goodbye.

I loathed them, their expensive clothes, their weak Googling. I loathed the bottled water they drank, how their plastic was probably collecting on coasts, how their houses and their gospels did not seem to match, how they'd never even met a Haitian and yet had drawn all these nasty, interrupting conclusions. I loathed that, to me, they represented the parts of my country that had exploited the other country that I loved so much; how their racism, privilege, and greed stood out, how it made mine stand out as well. I loathed that the pastor had never been to the island where he was sending me. That a new wing of the campus was being built and here I was tap dancing for lawyers and doctors just trying to get a new kitchen constructed at Papa's House so that the locals in Les Cayes might get to sell their own bread.

I had found a new group of people to blame for the wounds of the roadside man, and they were the white, evangelical, wealthy church folk whose tithes made possible my paychecks and tickets to do the good of the Samaritan on their behalf.

Their God-blessed greed (or the greed that they represented) had done so much damage to so many oppressed people
groups, exploiting weaker governments and darker skin. Their
ill-proportioned and excused power had been accepted if not
hidden for most of my life. And I was growing cynical about the
damage to people and land being caused by my country and religion's deals with the devil.

Alone in my car driving from that large church to the hospital, I rambled to myself about all of the American and Christian
history we had not been taught; and I wondered how our cen-
turies of exploitation might have added to the shifting of status
from son to orphan or the shifting of cells in my Aunt Kathryn's
body. My insides churned while we bought time, as people do in
waiting rooms, grouped into pods of familial worry and vending
machine snacks.

We were there for the big surgery. This was the major test
that would label our family's path either Stage 3 or Stage 4. This
was the road's fork that split the chances. The three younger kids
(my brother and cousins) joined the adults, among whom I now
sat, and asked again for information. I'd seen the looks around me
before, on porches waiting for storms.

With an open door and twenty-two eyes shooting towards
it, "I'm sorry," the doctor said, releasing the catapult of dread that
lasted for the entire next year of treatments and tears; the entire
next year of doctors' appointments, and smoothies, and visits from
old friends; the entire next year of morphine drips, and in-home-
hospice, and arrangements for Aunt Kathryn's girls. It lasted for an
entire year of "lasts" that will never be "nexts" ever again: a year of
letters, and suffering, and drawing close, and closing off.

I hung my black dress on my bedroom door for a month
before Aunt Kathryn passed just trying to stay in touch with reality. I'd stare at it from the red comforter of the full-sized bed in
my "big girl" apartment, chasing mental trails of which robbers
to accuse for what.

Her oldest was my cousin, pregnant with the first great-grand
baby who would come earth-side a short two months after Kathryn's

death. Her middle, grasping for grades in her freshman year away at college, paid for home visits with countless and costly study hours. Her youngest, still at home and sixteen, was left alone with paternal instability—no longer shielded by her saint of a mom.

Aunt Kathryn's funeral brimmed with bright flowers and people whom she had inspired; and if someone could have bottled the tears of those who were both celebrating a life well lived and mourning a life tragically lost, I feel that elixir could create a black hole of empathy able to suck the world into what really matters. Dragonflies lit on a cemetery full of dandelions while I noted how sorrow did not slam me like the freight train for which I'd been bracing. Instead, I'd been grieving in sporadic blows since the doctor first opened the door. They continue today, spaced between an increasing number of months.

The day that her presence just vanished off the earth and out of her home-hospice room, leaving only the relics of a chest of drawers and books, was the day that I obliterated the weak medicine of everything happening for a reason. It was easier to think about it all as an injustice: a disease caused by chemicals in land or water or food that were caused by materialism that was caused by people. Bad people. Robbing people. Distorted Jesus-people. A loss at the hand of a corporate sin over which Christ himself wept.

Otherwise, we lived in a world where God could just snatch loved ones up and tell those who remained not to bother trying to understand a plan that was not ours to comprehend. And I could stomach a God who mourned with us far more than a God who might strike for reasons never revealed—a God who was a robber himself.

Her letter to me was the last that she wrote before the Dilaudid took her sensibility.

"This is very difficult for me to go through," she said, "but I think I have almost reached the point where I know it's OK . . . I hope I am making sense baby, sometimes the tops of my legs hurt so bad . . . my fingers and hands are so numb that it's hard to write . . . I just really want you to know that I love you and you are a very special gift from God—that I have so enjoyed loving! I know that

God has big and amazing things planned out for you to do—but guess what? He may just choose for you to be a wonderful mother! That's a pretty amazing thing to be."

Her words, now more prophetic than ever, will never not be fresh. Cancer had robbed us and made us, shifted us all into being a family no longer unfamiliar with the palpable company of impossible grief, rich gratitude for fleeting time, and simmering anger for all of those who had functioned as the thief in this world. I was becoming mad at anyone whom I assumed had ignored the words of Jesus and stoked their greed by selling products that kill; who had closed their doors and borders; who had demonized the poor; who had supported politicians and pastors that were supporting factories that were killing God's good people and God's good earth.

I was becoming mad and also so scared that I might be living in a society where no number of Samaritans (and no number of hours becoming one) could keep me from the threat of pitch dark pain and loss.

The Earthquake

I had the sense about me to grab a notebook as some remaining logic inside of my head let out one last cry before being snuffed out again by the will to survive. "I may want to remember this," I thought.

Inside the one-subject pad—collected by Americans and intended for some child in the southern hills—I took notes all the way to the embassy. And that is right where I left them, along with all of my clothes and the rest of our possessions that threatened too much weight for our evacuating C15 cargo plane.

Four days earlier, we'd traveled the always-changing, bumpy dirt road through Port au Prince heading to the south of Haiti. It was a supply-dropping, project-scouting, information-gathering trip of three travelers—an in-between-teams-team meant to touch base and come right back home.

Since we'd arrived as a partner at the orphanage, gardens had been created yielding eggplants, pumpkins, okra, and peas. Eight latrines and showers had been constructed to offer greater hygiene. Dining pavilions, playgrounds, and teachers' storage had been installed to further flesh out the complex.

But for all of the progress, there were still things missing— gaps in the dots between Shreveport and Les Cayes. Money was not stretching like we thought it should be stretching. Kids were still looking sicker than we thought they should be looking. We'd arrived to bring more medicine, ask more questions, and conduct the impossible detective work of a few white foreigners only on the ground for a handful of days.

Who is the robber here? I would scan, picking up clues and suspecting lead pastors of turning childcare into cash cows. *I must find the poor robber here so that I can fix the poor robber here before the rich robbers back home feel victimized and validated in their suspicions.*

After some hours of popping in, prying, and swinging children into the air, we took that romantic drive back to the guest house. Teal water glittered through the palm fronds. Women with their strong necks held a week's worth of fruit on top of their braids. Piles of cassava bread would interrupt the stench of burning trash. Caribbean music, coral-washed houses, and potholes that would send us crashing into a vehicle's ceiling flew on by. Haiti in January felt like that one wonderful spring day that we get in the Deep South: pleasant. I was growing in comfort and confidence in-country, hanging on to a thread of hope that God still honored the willing with blessings of safety and the reward of a good story.

I pressed send on an email to update our organizations back home right as my laptop began to jostle back and forth. The bed, on which I sat resting barefoot at the end of our long day began shifting inch by inch. I looked toward the walls, speechless and confused by their jello-jiggly nature.

One of my traveling companion ran in from the bathroom, "Is this an earthquake?"

"I think this is an earthquake," I said. "Should we stand in a doorway?" I shot out as the only idea I could draw from what I once learned in those junior high natural disaster units.

"I think we should get out into the open," she advised. The cold stone of the staircase under my feet shook back and forth like a disorienting feature of a state fair's funhouse. The rest of the home's residents had congregated in the driveway, equally far from all trees and columns. I crouched low to the ground, four limbs attempting to steady like a quadrupedal animal while the earth trembled on and the most eerie and low noises traveled throughout the air.

Once the waves had ceased and we were confident enough to reenter the house to assess the cracks and lost connections, the question was proposed: *What if this wasn't the center?* And it wasn't.

"We should try and reach home . . ."

One by one our transmissions were checked off as inoperative. No Internet, no TV, no phone calls could connect. As a last attempt, a text was sent out into space as we pled for its landing.

"We are ok," it read.

"THANK GOD," we immediately received from our families right as all of Haiti went black.

What has happened? we shrunk.

That evening, we sat next to a TV whose makeshift, emergency antenna had been wired like a tower reaching as high as it could go for more information. Anderson Cooper peeked every now and then through the fuzzy black and gray static as we learned that a 7.0 quake had struck the most condensed area of the island a short ninety miles away from where we huddled around in fear and candlelight.

As the aftershocks continued through the night, rattling the remaining teacups in the cabinet, CNN told the world that Port au Prince had all but crumbled as recordings of screams and estimated casualties poured in. As night fell on the island, everyone was forced to accept that America (and therefore we) would know nothing more until the morning. I drew my covers up around my ears, attempting to block out the audible sounds of the earth groaning like a woman in pain, howling in low aching tones as everything shifted, and settled, and shifted again.

I ripped open my Bible with the edge of my flashlight like someone throwing their last coin in a well, and I asked for anything. *Give me anything.*

"For God alone my soul waits in silence, for my hope is from him. He alone is my rock and my salvation, my fortress; I shall not be shaken. On God rests my deliverance and my honor; my mighty rock, my refuge is God . . . Once God has spoken; twice I have heard this: that power belongs to God, and steadfast love belongs to you, O Lord. For you repay to all according to their work," I read in the sixty-second Psalm.

You are strong, and you love us. You have to be strong, and you have to love us. I held it like the small and lonesome hope that it was and fell asleep.

The morning met us disappointedly with little news or paths off the island, as did the next and the next and the next. The vehicles had been waiting their turns at the gas station since dawn and more news was coming in by way of neighbors' neighbors about schools collapsing, mass graves forming, and unfathomable displacement occuring. A satellite phone was finally located in town and I drank a cold Sprite while sobbing over my mom's voice on the Caribbean porch of a generous Madame and Misye.

"We're going to try and evacuate through the Dominican on Friday," I told my mother, attempting to steady my voice. "No news will be good news. I'll call you when we land somewhere." I was twenty-two.

The morning before we left our guesthouse with a pack of sandwiches, bananas, and water bottles, I took a permanent marker and wrote my social security number on my thighs, arms, and side. *Please just don't let me end up in a mass grave,* I prayed.

Our typical five-hour drive was multiplied by the steady stream of evacuees against whom we swam in our attempt to reenter the ruins being escaped, to get to a road that led to the country's western border where we would plead to be granted entry. The highways looked as if the gods had taken their outer edges, like a flat bed-sheet, and fluffed them right on up into the air, landing them back down crinkled, and smashed, and folded under themselves. We wondered what target we'd placed on our backs with our ice chests, filled tanks, and white skin. But the people kept redirecting us to open roads, pointing silently to each new way that we needed.

When we reached the city, the whole atmosphere felt like a panicked child trying to catch its breath. The concrete structures, bigger than two of my apartment complexes combined, sat in pieces, angled and resting against each other, towering above our vehicle like we were passing through the set of an apocalyptic movie. Making squares in the streets were bodies, dead and dust-covered, that had been drug out as boundaries for the living quarters of those who had now moved to the outside of their flimsy homes. I shot my head around to see the stiff arms of a man whose prostrate figure was being used as a stop sign laid across the dirt, his carcass now little more than a cry for aid workers to stop. I wanted to sob more than anything else, but my sorrow had locked itself away with my breath and my ability to process—things that would take months to return.

With our vehicle's gas petering after the extended trip, we were forced to redirect toward the American Embassy. "If you can get to the embassy, you'll get home," a kind stranger in the city had told us. "There are no promises out of the DR right now."

We stood in line for hours next to a soiled child with dysentery and her dirty, blood-covered father who had, just days before, watched the lives of his wife and other children be crushed in the rubble. They had simply been visiting. And now he was leaving with a fraction of his existence.

Who has failed you, I ached. *Who has robbed you? Who has robbed Haiti? Was it my people? Was it the greedy, high-heel bobbing Sunday school goer and generations like her? The pastors who were happy to function in dying churches? The risk-averse suburbanites? The right and left wingers all caught up in drawing lines? The racists?*

The homophobes? The people not loving like Jesus would love? Was it the politicians? Was it the church?

As supply planes emptied themselves and reloaded with evacuees who had been waiting for days, we scraped together abandoned blankets and made beds in the grass of the embassy's courtyard. When it came time to pass out MREs, our team volunteered as some of the only remaining able-bodied humans in the facility.

Rumors of tent cities forming and death tolls reaching the hundreds of thousands were circulating as I realized that once my feet left the Haitian soil, there would be no returning for a while. I was escaping a place that needed working hands and feet, escaping a place by way of a passport's privilege, escaping as someone completely and traumatically torn.

"If you have the strength to stand for hours and nothing more than a backpack, you may be able to fly out tonight. Come get in line," an authoritative woman in uniform commanded about ten hours after we arrived. In a pile with hundreds of other duffels, we threw our load. The cargo plane, like another prop in a movie, was surrounded by cots of UN and aid workers who had swiftly made the tarmac their new home.

Geraldo Rivera approached me with a microphone as I boarded to ask how I felt about finally getting out of the country. In my grief and exhaustion, I fought puking on him while noting how much shorter he was in real life and wondering how in the hell he'd gotten there so quickly. In disbelief, I stared in his direction as if he were a mirage likely to disappear into the dark and sad Haitian air.

"Tell the people I am angry," is all I wanted to say. Instead, I boarded in silence with the rest of my disturbed travel partners. US Air Force servicemen strapped us into their aircraft with its large back hatch closing in, and we flew into a makeshift displacement center in New Jersey where we were given hot showers, forms, and phone calls.

In a haze of unreality, we took a freezing train to Philadelphia, whose winter weather was inhospitable at best to the shorts and sandals we still wore from days before. Parting ways from our other evacuees, we waded through the airport surrounded by travelers who were not carrying the weight of fresh trauma. I picked up a magazine in a terminal cart that read, "Millions Homeless in Haiti with the Rainy Season Quickly Approaching," and I shook with the limitations of a broken body unable to produce tears.

Another publication questioned global warming, and my angry heart raged against the people, and their pollutants, and all the preachers who would say it was a warning for the wayward and wicked, and all the families who surrounded me in that moment heading out on their vacations.

The storms bring the rain; the rain brings the . . .

The rain brings . . .

Death.

More death that was natural, or consequential, or something . . .

More death that was painful, and ugly, and maybe avoidable.

More death that I couldn't wrap my mind around.

More death that was unjust, and undeserved, and unfairly unaccountable.

Who was to be held responsible?

Who?

Whisked away to my parents' home after the reporters and a crowd of God knows how many met us at the top of the Shreveport Regional escalator, I convulsed every time the news would flash scenes of Haiti's looting and violence. "But I saw the people, and they were helping each other," I'd wail, now mad at the filthy, lying news. And despite the loving eyes of my family assessing my every move and emotion, I felt as if I was in a desert.

I should have gone immediately into counseling. Instead, I got a tattoo that said "hope" in Kreyol and moved into a tent on the green space of my alma mater, asking people to join me.

"Come live in Tent City and raise money for orphan relief!" I advertised, still in shock. And folks were happy to gather. For seven days, students, families, businessmen and women camped out in the cold rain between their work hours and classes. At night, we'd huddle around a fire pit, sing songs, and pray. In the mornings, the news stations would cover our assembly and encourage people to drop money into our buckets for relief.

It was no compensation for whoever had inflicted (both historic and continued) wounds upon the Haitians while they walked their disaster-ridden road; but at least it was a small effort to not leave them there wounded. At least it gave my pain some small chance to move. At least it was an attempt to fix the robber's terrible mistakes and give our foreign friends the room and resources to become everything that they could be without the awful influence and hindrance of the place and people I called home.

Orphan Funeral

Having returned to Haiti some PTSD-saturated months later, the sound of a small hand bell rang from downstairs of the guesthouse. It was 8:04 and Danyis was letting us know that breakfast was ready. I solemnly made my way down the pink stairs, still cracked from the shakes of the year before; and I joined my team who sat in silence.

The day began with oatmeal made of half-and-half and cinnamon. A dollop of homemade, spicy peanut butter swirled around the middle. Fresh juice from the trees behind the guesthouse sat in a pitcher beside the white thermoses of hot chocolate and local, tar-black coffee. I grabbed hands of the travelers sitting to my right and left. It had been one thing to experience tragedy in a small group of visitors. It was now another to be there unable to stop it as the leader of a large team.

After breakfast, we trudged through the last half mile of Haitian mud on foot once our van had plonked itself down into two feet of sludge from the night's rainfall. Villagers dripped out of the mango trees into a second line following our somber march to the chapel. It was the rainy season, and we would be burying a child.

We'd arrived for another supply-drop trip a week before, similar to others we had made prior to the earthquake. Papa's House had the newest outdoor kitchen for miles and miles, and the damage left by the tremors and subsequent storms had been promptly repaired by the money raised by our church. Lovelie was sitting on top of one of the bunkbeds when we arrived with our army bags of medicine. She looked like life was leaking right out of her.

I did not often recognize my own intuition or trust any maternal instincts within me, but a feeling hit the back of my throat indicating that what had been alive was now dying. My gut contorted when I saw her; I knew she needed medical attention. We were maybe already too late.

The journey that followed felt impossible. Our team, which was piled high with trip veterans, carried about our intended business while another member and I spent the following week scurrying about the country's south side like mad women on a shortening timeline.

Why had she not been watched more closely? Where were the doctors that we were paying to visit? Where is the money going that we'd been wiring? Why can't I get any answers? Is there even a way to do this at such a long distance with no real, consistent presence on the ground? Is any of this even our role? Is any of it even good? This is so much more complicated than what I originally signed up for. It is not romantic. It is not fullest. It is not freest.

Over the next few days, I found myself at hospitals where women wore uniforms straight out of the 1950s and babies were birthed into chicken yards out front. I ate questionable fried pockets of meat while Lovelie, this weary four-year-old with no strength not to trust us, received blood work that would turn out to tell us nothing. We found ourselves in dark gray visa offices where big men in suits yelled words I couldn't translate fast enough.

"Is this what my grandfather's crowds were like?" I winced as they hollered about more money for rushed and not entirely legal paperwork.

We parked our truck at the edge of a barely navigable mountain two hours from town. And after crossing creeks and hiking almost vertical hills, we finally arrived at the three-sided lean-to, home of Lovelie's teenage mother and her three younger siblings. She signed the release papers for which we had argued back at the dark office, papers that would pave Lovelie's way to a Shriners hospital in the States; then she returned stoically to the daily task of finding food. I watched her whole body, trying to read her emotions. But nothing was discernible. Sometimes I think about her and wonder if emotional responses are themselves a privilege of those who think they have options when she knew that she didn't, that she never had.

I'd been reading Timothy T. Schwartz's *Travesty in Haiti: A True Account of Christian Missions, Orphanages, Food Aid, Fraud and Drug Trafficking* on the flight down. It was ruining me for the standard evangelical mission mentality. I was questioning the institution of orphanages and their history of corruption in the country. I was questioning the systems that we were possibly causing or perpetuating. I was questioning the pastors with whom we were working, the American partners with whom I had invested great trust, the legitimacy of food aid compared to the correlating stats of child mortality. I questioned every single contributor's intentions and actions, and I wondered if there was anything simple and clear in the world anymore. I wondered if there was a soul in the work of the church who could not be suspected of robbing.

Lovelie died the night before we were to head with her paperwork to the embassy, after every door for her passage to a Miami hospital had been shoved open by our network of people in-country and back home. Time stood still under the guest house's blue bug zapper as our translator explained through tears what had taken place the hour before; how she had taken one last deep breath that lifted her toddler chest into the air and back down again. As he spoke, I watched through the screen door as my team sat under a seashell chandelier, playing cards and laughing.

"We know that this is a part of God's plan," the translator said. I did not argue, though I wanted to. The potent suffering I had so recently witnessed made me unwilling to believe that God wanted this to happen any more than I did—at least, the God that I wanted to follow. The child's country had been stripped and exploited by more powerful governments; her care was subject to a lying partner; her parents were economically paralyzed because of a terrible lack in resources (or maybe they were merchants whose inventory got lost in the storms that were caused by greedy people's misuse of land, or maybe they were farmers whose crops spoiled to mush when the American policies changed the trade agreements or when the churches started piping in free rice and beans).

How would I tell them . . .?

How would we move forward . . .?

After all of this. After we prayed, how would we pray . . .?

The smallest casket I had ever seen rested unevenly on cinder blocks; and the eighty-two children bellowed with damp faces for their small, once lively sister.

I was thankful that we were there to pay for the funeral and offer thirty extra arms for rocking grieving kids. But it was then that I decided I no longer knew how to ask God for healing or safety in this big, wide, knotted web of suffering possibly caused by the selfish systems of other people. And I decided that foreign poverty work was no longer less complicated than domestic poverty work—I had simply, up until now, had the option of a return flight home to avoid the depths.

I was losing trust that helping was helping, and therefore I was also losing my passion and parts of my identity and theological constructs upon which everything else rested.

How Much Nothing I Felt

"Britney, there's someone here for you," the secretary buzzed. When I reached the bottom floor of the giant church's office space, a woman in a hospital gown looked my way, frazzled and preparing to spill what she had rehearsed (I assumed). I braced myself for the same old story.

"Hi, I'm the Missions Director. They said you needed to speak with me," I began.

"No ma'am, I didn't tell anyone anything; I just walked in. I'd like to pray with a preacher." Her eyes welled up. Embarrassed that I'd been summoned simply because of her clothes and not because of her request, I walked her to the second floor and slumped to my office thanking God that I didn't have to listen to one more exaggerated tale meant to sway my write-off of another assistance check.

For the first few months of my expanded job from foreign missions director to foreign and local missions director, I lived for each chance of being interrupted in my money-wiring and team-designing by a knock of need on our giant building's front door. I absorbed every story of abuse, of being jumped, of having lost it all in a fire, of just moving and losing jobs when the factory left town; and I wrote check after check for rent, and lights, and water. In the beginning—before the earthquake, and Lovelie, and the high-heel-bob of another sassy rich lady—I felt like Robin Hood. But things had shifted and were shifting still.

I'd leave my morning coffee cup to go stop by the bus station to get passes, or by Miss Johnson's house to discuss the painting we'd be doing the next Saturday, or by the shelter to drop off congregants' donations that we couldn't take overseas. But with no social work degree and functioning in a go-between role of a large, affluent, and hard to mobilize (for this twenty-three-year-old) congregation, I felt my heart corroding.

Standing as a link in the chain between pocketbooks and poverty was fine until I began to yearn for relationships beyond what felt like business deals. The hurt was so great and condensed in that front lobby every first of the month, but without a community to help shoulder the stories, to help process why there was such a big gap for which to be the chain's link, the work simply became heavy and transactional.

As I pulled back into the church parking lot after lunch one day, I parked my car and stared six rows over to see a man sitting, surrounded by torn Walmart bags full of dirty clothes, undoubtedly asked to wait outside for when I returned. In response to his presence, I turned my car back on and drove away, feeling nothing.

I felt nothing until I felt crisp, raw fear about how much nothing I felt.

I pulled in front of the downtown coffee shop, slid some quarters into the meter, and went in to hold my head alone at a table. Church work in this way was proving to be filled with such great divides between the haves and the have-nots and such large hurdles in bridging the two. I felt extremely conflicted about all the hullabaloo it took every year just to keep the lights on with faithful tithes while the closest neighborhood to the steeple (one in which few members lived) struggled as a food desert.

I felt extremely conflicted about my salary being a part of those elaborate stewardship campaigns. I wanted anyone to challenge anyone with any non-vague way of living like Jesus lived—enemy-loving, violence-absorbing, parable-crafting, least-of-these-humanizing, food-multiplying, walking with the poor, helping-without-hurting Jesus.

I loved church work. It was the only thing I had ever planned to do, the only thing I knew how to do since I walked that call-answering-aisle in Memphis. And yet—as the priest, the Levite, and the Samaritan roles all drew strikes through themselves—I didn't know where or how I could fit into it anymore. Not in this setting, in this way, with the suits and the slums passing each other in the lobby and it feeling like my sole responsibility to do the bidding for both.

A friend walked into the coffee shop, ordered her drink, and sat down beside my distinguishably disturbed demeanor.

"What's going on?" she asked.

"I feel like I'm losing . . . like I've lost . . . every bit of my passion. I just drove away from work because I saw a poor man sitting outside, and I didn't know if I could handle one more story alone."

Assuming she would comfort, validate, or excuse me, I waited with a look of *you know what I mean.* But then she said something that was more affirming than any of those other things could have been.

"Britney, this is tragic."

She was right. I cried. It was.

I'd grown to be so cynical and world-weary of most everyone with whom I was brushing shoulders on a daily basis. The orphanage pastors with their lack of information; the stateside partners with their defenses and jewelry; the inexperienced new travelers with their idealized outlooks; the church staff in all of its soiled functioning; the congregation with all of its blindness; the poor folk with all of their need; the American Christians, and their concert stages, and their stories that felt like they had nothing to do with anyone's actual life; the American Christians and their land exploiting and people ignoring, their reluctance to be real neighbors to neighbors, their distaste for deep and holy community. And me, stretched between them all, unsure of who or where to be.

She was right, it was tragic. And I was grateful to hear that it was tragic. That meant that someone thought that it didn't have to be tragic. And there may yet be another world in which to reside, another way to live out faith that wasn't so transactional and corrupt.

I had to redirect before the waters of what felt like unfaithfulness overtook me and forever made me into the church employee that I so desperately couldn't let myself become: burnt-out, compassionless, and complicit.

Let's Move

On one of our last Haiti trips as an annually returning group of twenty-somethings, we'd stuffed our stomachs full of plantain, piklis, and Prestige beer and climbed into the back of that railed Toyota to return to the guest house for packing. We'd enjoyed an evening at the beach with hammocks and small crabs, murky ocean and lime green driftwood, rest and pictures and recapping before wrapping our trip.

There were no city lights to dilute the crystals that had been spread like jam across the black Caribbean sky. There were no cell phones to keep our heads down, no seat belts to hold our bodies in. One team member stood to his feet with his opened, button-up church shirt dampening at the edges from his wet swimsuit. He outstretched his arms and let the island wind whip around him as it did for the hawks and thrushes.

Another member, jealous of the sensation, grabbed his T-shirt by the neck-seam and ripped it right down the middle to begin flying as well. We laughed while holding hands and resting on shoulders, spent in all the realistic and informed ways—no longer delusional island newbies. It was one of the most deliciously hippy moments of my entire life.

For all of the grief to which I had been introduced over the previous few years, I still felt free in Haiti when I was with my friends. I felt free within a community of people who had drawn close. There are few instances, before or after, that I remember feeling as perfectly alive—surrounded by hands that made light the heavy load that we now knew all too well.

Our prayers, daily routines, possessions, sorrow, growth, dinner table, and efforts for service had all been shared while we were there together, every time. So we knew community was possible, and if it was possible, then it was maybe possible for more of life to feel alive than in just those scrapbook moments of travel. New Monastic authors seemed to think it was possible. Commune dwellers seemed to think it was possible.

But here we would be, returning yet again to what felt like uncompelled and isolated living—separated into our own gated apartments, enslaved to our technology, and bills, and the hustling we did to pay them, sixteen-hundred miles away from any poor people that we could say with good conscience that we knew and loved, and all of us—every person—owning toasters. There were a dozen toasters between us when we'd seen how capable we were of sharing just one.

Someone opened up a box of Pop-Tarts when we arrived back at the guesthouse after that last drive, while someone else opened up their Bible to the second chapter of Acts to read about the first church and how they lived so interwoven and intentionally.

Were we ready? To do it? To live together and among the poor? Ready to sell off our stuff because we no longer needed six washing machines? Ready to see Jesus's words more consistently and tangibly than in the annual mission trip markers or in our stale, dead pews? Were we ready for a holistic faith that asked things of us: faith that expected intentionality in our home and our money, in our politics and our pantries, in our confession, and learning, and waste, and our concept of church?

No, was the truth. We were not ready.

But we thought we were, so we did it anyway.

The answers and the actions—when they were nowhere else—now had to be found in New Monastic community, I'd concluded. Hope had to be somewhere. And this was the only thing, in a whole host of nonsensical other things, that made any sense now. It would be how we would renew the land that was groaning in quakes and carcinogens. It would be how we would become friends with people who were really in need and leave in our dust those who just spent their time complaining and concluding about the poor.

It would be how we would shoulder together such big grief and complexities, how we would make the world better by living closely and with integrity—no longer a Robin Hood in the faith, now finally a neighbor. No longer just a Samaritan passing through a road filled with nasty, terrible robbers, but an innkeeper there to stay.

6

Communal Living

The Innkeeper

These floors that you sweep, the cups that you offer and wash, the ever-evolving system you create and abide by to decide who gets to stay and who doesn't, a revolving door and a stable foundation: this is all your home—your shared home.

Digging into your satchel, you scoop up a heaping handful of grain to scatter amongst the chickens in the courtyard. They worry not about the cracks in the mud-brick walls or the age of the roof's straw above—not like you do. The undertaking of this place is much more extensive than what your dreams led you to believe all those years ago when your belly first burned at the idea of an inn. But the always full table makes it a little more worth it than not. The inconceivable rarity of the conversations you've been able to witness over the years is not lost on you.

Once the cistern has been checked and the fire stoked, you've just about ascended the ladder to the upper level when a fraught voice hails from the entrance. Your skin has somehow both softened and thickened with the time that it's spent making a home with open doors; learning the

*boundaries, and then crossing them, and then sometimes
erasing them altogether. Hospitality has taught you that
there are few hard lines, only day-by-day discernments.*

*"Hello!" you hear again. "Please, somebody help us!"
It is one of the cries you've rarely been able to ignore, not
like the midday door rappings of the mundane neighbors
that you sometimes tune out.*

*For no more than two seconds, you are taken aback
by the shared company of a Samaritan and his Jewish
invalid (parties who would typically strive to avoid each
other). But this stone archway has served as an entry point
for more bizarre assortments than this.*

*He's likely dead, but you'll do what you can. This
is why you built this lodge in the first place. It seems the
world may never stop spitting folks out onto roadsides, and
you felt it was right to make sure that there would always
be beds in which to catch them and bodies of people in
which to enfold them.*

Beds and broth and bodies—a community for all.

The Yellow House

OUR FILTHY ISLAND CLOTHES had barely been washed before we
began clocking out of work and driving the blocks of Highland
looking for a house into which our whole crew could move. It
needed to be rentable or a purchase process laced with miracles.
And it needed to be big enough for seven twenty-somethings who
were interested in doing *a thing.*

The neighborhood of Highland was an enigma. We learned
quickly that the western side was known as one of the more astute
areas of town while the north was a hodgepodge of quirkiness and
poverty. It was considered an at-risk district with a high crime rate,
a good number of low-income households, and more diverse skin
and language than many other parts of the city. It was filled with
homes who had yet to graduate any family members from high
school, first-generation English speakers, young hipsters making
art, and college students looking for cheap rent. Depending on the
block, one section could be known for its sexual predators or meth

addicts on parole while another might be known for its upper-middle-class families moving in to renovate historic homes or counter the city's sprawl. It was a mixed bag for us newcomers, to say the least—an eccentric place of pride and history.

The large yellow house on the corner of Dalzell and Gilbert became ours the summer after we met a military family in town who said that they had felt God telling them that they were supposed to buy it for us. We took it to be the makings of a grand story: this relationship forming between a conservative B2 bomber pilot and a bunch of young maybe-pacifists who lacked a mission statement for their wild vision of a modern, progressive, Christian community. I have rarely seen generosity as quick and abundant as that of the Free Family, who opened their lives, their crockpot, and their savings account for such an abstract and zealous movement. Their gift and trust made it feel like God was on our side.

We trickled in as residents after our separate leases ended, and we spent all non-working hours doing whatever renovations we could afford while figuring out how we might think about what we were actually becoming. The front lobby was aged and mismatched as if several attempts had been made to give it an identity. The door of our former halfway house swung open on its own when released from the lock. And the lopsided walls soon confirmed the abysmal state of the foundation.

A set of tiny bronze keys were replicated and dispersed as the air filled with particles from the floor sanding we were attempting ourselves. A spry leaf the color of limes dropped down to eye level, thwacking all who entered with an eager welcome. It led to a vine that led up the ceiling, around a door frame, and into a hole where cats were getting in. The sound of gunshots would bounce around the acoustics of that eighty-year-old home as our new homeless friends would attempt to break in, highlighting our growing need for the security system we could not afford. Meanwhile, our new place, our new intentional community, had no working HVAC and the hottest Louisiana months in over a hundred years were settling in around a web of electrical wiring that struggled to support the infiltration of window units.

As young twenty-somethings, we felt all things fleeting and urgent. Accordingly, we neglected to make any travel efforts to spend learning time within groups of people who were living the very lives that we'd been inspired to chase. Therefore, in and amongst the wall painting and the floor sealing, the hole patching and the heat escaping, the job-holding and the school finishing, the door-locking and the noise-assessing, we were constantly discussing what we were going to do, who we were going to be, and what difference it was all going to make. Additionally, we were being drilled by our anxious families with questions about how it all pertained to our degrees and what we would do with this couple's newly acquired debt if we all got married and moved.

"But we won't," I'd assure. We were the innkeepers. We were all there to stay, for the long haul, forever.

And people would donate to this worthy cause, and pay our debt, and fund our efforts like they'd donated to all the other worthy causes I'd been fortunate enough to be a part of. We just needed to give them the opportunity.

So we threw a party, invited all the neighbors, businessmen, teens in poverty, and twenty-somethings that we knew. We called it a kingdom-on-Earth style banquet and positioned ourselves for another financial blessing.

It only took one humiliating moment of sharing this muddy dream with a crowd of people for me to realize how long I had been functioning in the Christian culture of "do good and people will pay your way." Our guests, while pleasant, were more willing to ask the well-founded questions about our ideas than they were to open their pocketbooks. But I had grown to expect financial provisions for "faithful" ideas, grown to shame those who wouldn't buy into them as *unfaithful* and stingy. I'd grown into the entitled missionary that I'd not expected I could become.

That evening whisked up a few small bills and a whole lot of confusion that had to be quickly deflected as we huddled around the long, sticky kitchen island at the end of the night.

"Maybe God would not bless our efforts for a community house until we shifted our efforts toward the community within the house," someone suggested.

"'You expected much, but see, it turned out to be little. What you brought home, I blew away. Why?' declares the Lord Almighty. 'Because of my house, which remains a ruin, while each of you is busy with your own house," someone read from Haggai 1:9.

"It must be a lesson in prioritizing our shared life above a comfortably completed home; a lesson in making sure that our priorities rest on our relationships and not in our renovations," we concluded.

Resolving that we could do very little to speed up the process of a major overhaul, we set our intentions on hovering over window units, taking care of what was free (our connections), and praying to God for what was not.

We tucked, rolled, and chunked the disgusting crimson carpet over the balcony. We plucked the zealous vine as far back as it would go, set the pink doors on the curb, removed the cats every time they intruded, and picked up buckets of glass from the backyard. We hammered down nails, and scrubbed, and bleached, and swept (and swept, and swept, and swept). We cut down dying trees blocking sunlight from the future garden, painted halls, rooms, and trim. We sanded and stained floors during the midnight hours and asked, with far less worry than the situation merited, what we had gotten ourselves into.

It was exciting. If it was not yet settled intentional community, it was so very exciting. We'd become self-glorified house flippers who were bringing our experiences from Haiti (and what we'd read about New Monasticism) to the "destitute" neighborhood of Highland . . . eventually . . . surely . . .

And though still lacking a mission statement and really any time to establish the rhythms that would shape one, the house began to feel a bit more like a home when the coffee was being made in the mornings and suggestions of chore charts had begun to circulate. And though they were still unaware of why we existed, our neighbors began using the space over time as well.

We hosted weddings, wakes, and baby showers. We dropped cookies off at Pat's place three houses down and the next week found a pan of her homemade mac and cheese on our doormat. A need would find its way through hearsay to our couches, and we'd scramble up the money between us to get someone new tires or a few counseling sessions.

Worship music would break out around our dinner table every now and then, and we made a lot of art that became statement pieces for who we hoped we were becoming. Once a week, cathartic confession was practiced in the living room for the first time since college; and we said a lot of things like, "I've never told anyone this," and "Me too," and "Let's pray."

Attempting to become the official, intentional, Christian community that our new website said we were before anyone could get too discouraged or doubtful, efforts were made to add programs to our already full plates that would make us more genuine. A massive garden was built (though we'd taken no time to learn about gardening). A weekly block party was started; and prayer walks, trash pickups, game nights, teachings, meals, and hospitality rooms were all initiated in the slivers of space and energy that we had left from our otherwise unchanged schedules.

And though burnout was blowing its warning horn through constant fights over dishes and personality clashes, my roommates were beginning to feel like my family. They were my people and that house, my home. It was becoming my neighborhood during the season of young adulthood (especially as a single person) when home felt like a concept not allowed to be mine. Our community of people was becoming the place to which I could return, folks with which I could share the details of my daily life and my wonderings about the world and our role in it.

Fewer Places to Hide

I often missed our old apartment and not sweating like a soaked sponge from my scalp while making coffee, while showering, while sleeping. I missed not fretting about the noisy streets and the large risks we had all taken, floating "out here on our own" as it felt. The inner city made me miss the calm, which made me miss the country more than anything.

But Highland had porches, pedestrians, and parks with southern pines that stretched out over straw-covered yards in the fall. And those were nice perks to the sacrifice that was living downwardly mobile, which I loosely understood at the time as "we could be elsewhere, but we're choosing not to be; and somehow this lifestyle is leveraging for the poor."

We'd park in the back beside the old plywood shed that we'd spruced with a bright coat of barn-red paint; and we'd use the kitchen door that was able to be pried open with a mere pocket knife when we'd forget our seven copies of bronze house keys. One evening—instead of popping open the backdoor to find Max, a resident at the time, posted against the stove learning how to poach eggs like he'd been practicing for a while—we found a cold, dark bottom floor.

A lamp-light angled out from the back bedroom where Max was lying face down on his small rug, sulking and shame-ridden next to a packed suitcase, a letter in his hand. "I cannot stay, you do not want a monster in this house," was the sentiment of the note that was passed between the housemates who were now sitting cross-legged around the drama of his outstretched body.

This is all I've done; this is all that has ever been done to me. Here are the ways I have tried to redeem myself and all the instances that make me think I may just be irredeemable. I am a cancer to this body, an appendage you must sever.

Once the letter had circulated and it became obvious that he'd braced himself for removal, a community member rose silently to her feet, unzipped the resting, waiting suitcase, and began to place his clothes back onto emptied shelves.

"Nice try," she said as the group took a breath. "But you're not special enough to be the only one with doubts, and a past, and real beef with God and God's people in this home. You're not the only one in need of that slow, painful peeling up of the scabs that hide the heart's wounds."

Close living with shared purpose and a good bit of self-awareness work (here's the predictable shout out to the Enneagram you've been waiting on) would prove to do that to folks over the next set of years. It happened every few months like clockwork; like bittersweet goodness. Like gold being driven through the fire, the stuff we thought had just become a silent part of who we were would start to bubble right on up to the top when there were fewer places and hours in the day to hide from one another. It felt as if a richly safe space was being created for people to work out their salvation within beloved community.

Safe Place

In the way that my dad's Aunt Martha's living room always felt mostly beige and our old church sanctuary felt mostly basil green, the highest room in the community house always felt mostly cobalt. It was cool, and cobalt, and tucked away where all of the hardest conversations would happen.

Mary had requested we talk after morning prayer one day, and no amount of experiencing months of dim rooms and confrontation could prepare my heart for not recoiling to the back of my ribs when someone would ask to meet.

I'm being called into question . . . I've hurt someone . . . Someone needs something of me that I can't give . . . I would fight in my brain.

"I just wanted you to know that I'm gay," she said the words we'd eventually end up hearing several times over before the house would close its doors.

Be cool, I thought. *You're being entrusted. Be cool, you're not who you were. You're not the Levite on the other side of the duct-taped line.*

"Thank you for sharing that with me; I know you didn't have to. I want you to know that this is a safe place," I said, wanting that aspect of our inn to be so true.

I wanted us to be making a place where people could hammer out their own lives as Max, the others, and I were hammering out ours. I wanted us to be making spaces that were dedicated to a few anchoring things: morning prayer, shared food, discussions about Scripture, peace, and hurting as few people in as few ways as possible (which had now become the theology of our collective moral compass). Dedicated to getting closer to God, pointing folks in God's direction, and then letting God tell them what was and was not desired for their lives felt like far greater a tactic for sanctification than legalism and rule imposition. If pressed, I still didn't have many answers for the ins and outs of homosexuality and faith. But for a freeing, first time in my life, I didn't feel like I had to. There were more important things.

"For who?" she said, batting my proud inclusion to the floor. "For you? For difference? For people who are working it out? Who are willing to have questions?" I stammered. "It doesn't feel safe to me," she said calmly.

I froze, demonstrating my lack of confidence. I reached deep for what the discipline of conflict among a house full of young adults had attempted to build within me over the year: be teachable.

"Can you explain more?" I asked, speaking like a listening person in the hopes of maybe one day being one.

"People are praying for the sexuality of kids in their youth groups as we sit around the candles each morning. There's an underlying assumption that the overall consensus is that a faithful lifestyle is not a gay one. The very language of everything is heteronormative and masculine at that," she suggested, running a highlighter though the parts of our days that I, in the blindness of my straightness, could not see.

"I'm sorry," I said, smooth responses depleted. I recognized that she was not approaching me with a part of herself to be worked out, but rather a part of herself that she had already worked out within her own faith as what she believed to be designed and sanctioned by God. She wasn't looking for my opinion, she just wanted to be able to be all there when she was there; all there in a space that was becoming hers like it was becoming mine.

"We really are trying. Or, we really want to be trying. I really want to be trying." I said, defenses finally down.

"I know you are," she smiled.

What I learned that day, in the cobalt room, was that it would need to be those who needed to feel safe who indicated whether a place was safe or not. Just because we had deemed it as such, in all of our hopes of inclusivity, did not mean that we held the perspective to inform actual inclusivity.

Could we make a place where people could grapple with varying theologies, dedicated to not controlling each other's positions in the journey? Could the guy who came to the weekly Bible study believing that acting on his same-sex attraction was altogether unfaithful for him have the same room as the woman who had long ago made peace with it as a beautiful, faithful existence for her? Could they both have the same room as the heterosexual evangelical who didn't really have a dog in their fight but maybe did (or didn't) want to learn more?

The doing, for this innkeeper, now rested primarily in the cultivation of a living room that could hold all the questions instead of being a body that could know all the answers. The doing was in the listening and not controlling; it was in the connection and not the image; it was in the careful crafting of words as to not ostracize or further wound.

I began to think a lot about the argument that words were just words—the argument I had long supported in my college years when I felt like all those liberal Christians were forcing the mincing of mine, promoting a culture of over-sensitivity, forcing folks to walk on eggshells. "People are too thin-skinned about the things that others say," I'd campaigned.

But I was learning that most powerful things were equally capable of great goodness and great harm—like humans, like risk, like water, like gifts. And words, being intrinsically powerful since the beginning of existence, had built me more than anything else, broken me more than anything else.

They'd changed me. More than anything else.

Our words, I was realizing in that drafty room on the third floor of the Yellow House, were gifted tools of life and death. And we couldn't shame people for taking them seriously, for feeling the weight of them being spoken or withheld, intended or not.

And when a bearer of God's image was so brave—or generous—as to share that the presence or absence of our words had left them less room in the community's circle, it became important to learn how to listen and not categorize the moment as less than a gift.

I was beginning to feel like this posture was possibly not one of diluted faith that "no longer thought the rules were important." But rather, the important rules were changing from being solely about behavior management and dogma clarifying to consistently getting and sitting closely, daily prayer, shared food, loving discussion; ears to hear over words to speak.

What an opportunity it was to not have to wait until marriage (if marriage was in the cards) to be seen and known, held and not deserted, stretched in love; to belong to each other, honest truth and all; to learn the deep waters of friendship's covenant; to make promises and spaces that meant something; to share conversations that challenged us and that would shape how we would live, or try to live, or miss living in the years to come.

Marriage

And just as I began to fall in love with our version of communal existence, just as I had begun learning about the possibility of making a larger home than the "my four and no more" future that I had been longing for since I was young, Luke came into my life, and we started talking about marriage.

He was different than the mental shrine of a partner that I'd built and worshiped in my youth.

Theologically conservative and morally liberal (in how I defined morals at the time)—my opposite. He was more corny than witty, more calculated than adventurous. He hated my *Friends* reruns, and I thought his *TedTalks* couldn't be more drab. He was not the worship leader I'd been searching for, and I was not the film student he'd hoped to find. But we could talk for hours, and he didn't mind crying in front of me, which I thought was a pretty good sign of a tender heart.

I'd been looking for so many years for a mirrored male version of me to whom I might hitch my wagon, that when Luke came along (with all his details to my impulse, his anchoring to my jumping, his benefit-of-the-doubt-giving to my frustrations, his gentle to my loud, his research to my ideals, and his logic to my whimsy), I almost missed him.

Then, he held me during funerals, and built the frames for my paintings, and bought the house across the street from the Yellow House just to be close and supportive. And those things seemed like they were becoming the most significant attributes I never thought to want. He hoped to be better, and make the world better, and was kind—which turned out to be pretty important criteria for partnership. He was becoming the string to my kite which made soaring possible; I was learning that tethering was good for flight, that function was good for vision, and limitations good for freedom.

But my college roommate's psychologist father had told us years before, as we pined away for lovers in our dorms, that we should live our lives in such a fulfilled way that someone would have to pry us out of singleness for marriage; that the notion of marriage should be entertained only if we could imagine that our partner would multiply our contributions to the world and God's work rather than diminish them. I'd found—and was building—a life of communal interdependence across the street from Luke that was hard to imagine leaving, even if just to move a mere fifty yards over.

I was now scared that a house of only two people would be the first step towards a life of only two people. But we tried, with as many words that we could formulate, to promise ourselves and our future marriage to a different way of living. We tried, with as many words that we felt optimistic about using, to promise to always be the innkeepers of the story.

Luke asked me to marry him at the bottom of the Yellow House staircase with sixty of our closest friends and family surrounding us with phone cameras and goofy smiles that made my face get a nervous twitch at its edges. Instead of a unity candle, we had a letter box resting on the altar at our wedding for friends and family to deposit nice words and prayers into our vows. I walked down the aisle to a song I'd written for Luke whose lyrics said, "Let's take our letter box; build us an obscure home; create a world that nobody's ever known." Our community and neighbors were there to dance the night away.

Moving just one house over, and painting walls, and creating our recipes, and ditching our rom-coms and documentaries for our jointly beloved sci-fi, and thinking on dreams that did and did not include the folks across the street was so special and so scary. My growing pains made me worry that the tides might be turning and that I had added to the turning.

And surely, they were, and I had.

Change Lanes, and Fast

In the irony of it all, just as the group of Yellow House residents had found a freedom of non-romantic yet intimate belonging, one by one more housemates began to date, become engaged, and look for starter homes in better school districts, just as twenty-some-things might be expected to do. And boom: the narrative changed before I could grasp that the changing was even possible.

We tried for a while to fill the emptying rooms with willing college grads and a structure that might compensate for the years of bonding that had first built the place. But a house meeting a week—which I would walk across the street to attend—compiled of new strangers and old friends, just could not produce the intentional atmosphere that would get newcomers up to speed before they too were contemplating a move.

Things were quite lonely if not unclear for all involved with such illusions of stability during life's most transitional season. Few things are sadder than being lonely in what people are calling a community house. Like feeling invisible in a congregation, one might wonder more than ever, "If I cannot feel loved, wanted, and connected here in this place that exists for connection, maybe I cannot feel loved, wanted, and connected anywhere."

My well-paying megachurch job now stood in a growing and undeniable contrast to the rest of my world that I'd begun loving and losing simultaneously. I was beyond tapped for the ability to make nice with funders, collect nonsensical donations, interpret the actions of partners for distanced congregants, and walk those stairs even one more time to have one more empty transaction with a desperate soul. I just wanted to be with my neighbors (who were still largely strangers) and my friends (who were now making different plans like I had made different plans). I just wanted to be sharing guesthouse life, all simple and spun together for the rest of time.

The night that the last new resident told me she'd be moving at the end of spring, following in the footsteps of everyone who'd first received keys and all the in-betweeners that came after, I walked back to our home office, slammed my back against the door, and slid to the ground in a flurry of "redirect or crumble." We had to change lanes, and fast, or it would all fall apart.

We had to change lanes, and fast, or sell the house a short two years after we'd first painted its white walls, bought its new refrigerator, and made all that cheap and easy spaghetti for each other. We had to change lanes, and fast, or lose that precious vision of another world and another way of existence that had become *the* way. It had become the only way: this way of the innkeeper. We had to change lanes, and fast, or crumble into the mediocrity of American, middle-class, evangelical living. We were almost out of options, I knew, for the radical existence for which I'd been searching since I was the seeker. Almost.

Options

One street and one alley over from the Yellow House was a home for neighborhood teenagers into which they could flood all energetic and perspiring after school each day for tutoring, art, and warm food. In the second floor at the time lived a family whose employing nonprofit valued the reality of its ministers being residents rather than visitors to a neighborhood. They had become a part of Highland: our kind of people.

We met them a little too late for partnership and just in time for appropriation—just in time to see a way out and a way forward for a dissipating ministry.

"There may be hope for us yet, what with a little more structure, a little more commitment, a little more time, and one more chance," I would rattle off to Luke at night. I asked the organization to hire me, to absorb our community house and entrust me to build their young adult program by building ours. I asked them for room to establish an internship out of the groundwork we had laid.

Still holding hope for what could be, a former housemate and I came onto their staff to build and fill a residential internship in intentional living. A "Twelve Marks of New Monasticism" curriculum was developed, dedicated college students and graduates (and their raised, missionary-style funding) were solicited, and a grant was received that paid off all of our impossibly daunting debt. It felt like the biggest of signs.

A rhythm of morning prayer and half-days of house meetings, neighbor visits, book studies, and practical application of practical good news was established. Completing the circuit, as Luke and I packed up our house and moved into the youth house the alley over when its former family left for Oklahoma, Yellow House interns became our built-in program helpers and our closest and dearest friends and neighbors.

We had standardized, but we had not dissolved. Lines had blurred, and maybe intentions compromised, but some version of the vision had not died. We had been afforded an opportunity to change it, maybe even deepen it, definitely follow it into what it was becoming: a systematized version of shared life in which we could all still be made new and faithful in the inn that had not yet closed.

Sarah (the other original Yellow House resident) and I were teaching as we were learning, taking part in what we never fully got to do with our peers as we were creating an experience for those who were younger. Excel files showed our focuses for the months and weeks, down to the hours of an intern's devoted year.

Novices

Some days—after an intern would return from their mornings of part-time employment at coffee shops or churches—were for house meetings for revisiting the residential covenant that had been signed prior to move-in. It stated everyone's willingness to be honest and kind and to not have marijuana or assault rifles in the house. Passive-aggressive folks practiced talking about how the undone dishes made them so gosh-darn angry, and aggressive folks learned about their susceptibilities in manipulation and room-commanding. The chore chart was glanced over, and sometimes, somebody would share a breakthrough in their grieving, or their praying, or their self-discovery.

On other days, we visited neighbors, inviting shut-ins, single moms, and aging, smoky-lung social workers to join us for prayer or for an upcoming block party. We'd plant flowers for widows or pick up old juicy trash from the broken sidewalks. We'd watch Ms. Penny wither with cancer; and we'd be shunned by people who just could not imagine, in this day and age, that our knocking was not a threat of invasion or religious conversion (or was it?). We never normalized the odd and uncomfortable feelings of trotting up the front steps of a stranger's home and explaining our unusual intentions of friendship (or neighborhood fixing). But we at least learned to embrace the discipline of door-knocking and the commitment to at least trying to learn the names of those living around us.

Book studies were a big part of our lives as well, and we'd take turns talking through our changing arsenal of literature meant to bring a human out of stagnant, judgmental evangelicalism and into the transformational reality of a faith that was good news for everyone. Later in the weeks, we would focus on little experiments that paralleled the twelve New Monastic marks (such as hospitality to the stranger, peacemaking amidst violence, and lament for racial divisions and the active pursuit of reconciliation).

In August, we'd host a racial reconciliation panel, in October we'd try our hand at Lectio Divina prayer. In November, we'd carry every bit of trash that we would typically throw away in a backpack just to see how much waste we were producing. In February, we'd write letters to people on death row. We'd handwash clothes, and deliver peppers, and choose to make Christmas gifts rather than buy them. We'd ride our city's bus system through poor neighborhoods in order to better understand the inefficiency of transportation for those who lived around us.

We'd paint murals with local teens and visit the landfill every year to lament its growth. We'd host pastor discussions addressing concerns and support of the local church, visit migrants at borders, and write cards to other communities to spur them on in this lifestyle that we knew to be both beautiful and hard. We'd march for peace when the gunshots felt out of control, and alter litanies and hymns to be more inclusive or to speak to the current injustices we were witnessing.

We'd play a lot of card games, and read Martin Luther King Jr.'s "Letter from a Birmingham Jail," and attend town hall meetings about environmental pollution and public school closings. If believing did not eventually look like doing, we'd started to wonder what we were actually believing in. If doing did not eventually look like stability and close proximity, like the innkeeper, we'd started to wonder if the doing was actually doing anything sustainable at all.

Most evenings were for teaching math, plating food, and playing games at the teen-house while weekends were sometimes for watering the tomatoes, for rest, and processing the ways we were all changing our minds and our habits.

We were changing our minds and habits pertaining to how the gospel of Jesus had to *now* always be heading toward real alleviation and restoration for the lonely, hungry, sick, or oppressed; how New Monastic, intentional, missional, faithful living meant that we could all really get better; that there wasn't a secret, or a need, or a church, or a system that couldn't get right if we all got close and contemplative, truthful and willing.

I could not imagine a better or different way of life. It became what I wanted for every single person in the world; it was what I wanted for our family for the rest of our livelong days. It was what I wanted for the church, across the board, in all contexts: a deep, free, connected, holistic and faithful, communal existence. For everyone, I wanted a life that could save us from our pious priesthood, our loose Levitical lifestyle, our short-lived Samaritanism, and the ruinous realities of those rich, rich robbers.

I had found the way that I had been seeking for so long. And like a blood oath with my neighborhood, I promised it the life of the innkeeper similar to a monk's most devout vows.

For Everyone, Forever

A week before Jonathan arrived, I sat in our office at the youth-house, cutting the recycling symbol out of a piece of computer paper to spray paint its rotating arrows onto a white trashcan. If one of New Monasticism's teachers was to be among us, at least it would be incentive for me to move my own personal practice of creation care further along. I was nervous to not be what I really needed us to be; I was nervous that his visit would indicate just as much.

Jonathan Wilson Hartgrove's books about applied faith, racial reconciliation, close Christian community, and deliberate life among the poor and the enemy had been formative for me and our life in the neighborhood. He had given concise language to so many inner wars and wonderings of mine over the seven years leading up; and I was restocked with new and fresh gratitude for the fact that I was getting to live and learn during the same era of faith as him and those like him.

He met and shared with many in our community and greater city during his visit. And while much stuck out during the discussions, I noted a common question floating around the rooms in which he sat. It was not foreign to us. It was one we'd asked and been asked many times in our previous five years of attempting to grow a life of intentional Christian community.

"Was New Monasticism for everyone?"

I sat near Luke, legs crisscrossed in our crowded bottom floor waiting for his answer.

Yes, I coaxed with my mind. *Say it. Say that it is. Say that it is the church's answer like I know that it is the church's answer. Say that it is where we're all headed. Say that what we are chasing so hard after is the calling of all people, everywhere. Say that this could translate, say that it should, to all seasons, all colors, all vocations. Say that it is the way to eternal life.*

"No," he answered. "I suppose that it's not."

My breathing shortened and I hoped my expression wouldn't give my panic away so freely.

"Monasticism has always been intended to point people toward Christianity, not toward monasticism." His answer was short. My security was rattled.

I sat with the conversation heavily for a week following. The question had been no stranger to my own thoughts; but I did not like Jonathan's answer on any level. I did not like that he had offered it so casually. And I wondered obsessively, what would have been my answer? What must it be to keep this worldview all intact before it threatens to unravel again?

New Monasticism had been a tool and structure that had given words and practical challenges in which my faith could be real, connected to, and informed by the world where we lived. Its marks had been a guidance for the transformation of this Sunday school Christian into one that thought her following of Jesus should have something to say to the various hurts of the earth: like poverty, systemic racism, war, isolation, fear, the death penalty, how we spend our money, creation care, and disconnection of the wealthy, etc. God had indisputably used its measures to show me that this life of discipleship had something to say about how we eat together, share our possessions, argue well, give unreservedly, and live closely. I had never felt more like a real follower of Christ and the implementing of his earthly example before it.

But, was it for everyone?

And if it wasn't for everyone, how could it be so perfectly for me?

Was this lifestyle of taking some of the most longstanding mo-nastic practices and applying them in the more marginalized places of our modern society in fact not for all people? Did any of the marks (or implementations) of New Monasticism that recent theologians and practitioners had outlined reside outside of the reach of any person's lifestyle or season (barring a bit of sacrifice)? Did these twelve practices, written to help laypeople model the ancient ways of monasteries, indeed work for all?

I wanted to say what Jonathan didn't say. I wanted to say yes. I wanted to say that what had so significantly changed and informed my life was accessible and intended for everyone else—like the sentiments shared by anyone whose soul has been so altered by a traveling preacher, a powerful retreat, or a mountaintop experience like Peter, James, and John, who witnessed Jesus glow like a ball of fire before them.

"We'll make tents and live here, Lord . . ." I knew the sentiment well.

I ached to camp out in the arena that had most transformed me, legalizing and manufacturing its principles. I wrestled, in the days after Jonathan left, wondering if I had been unrealistically hell-bent on my fixation with getting us all doing the same thing.

Was New Monasticism for everyone?

I no longer knew. But I needed to think that it could, at least, be for anyone.

I needed intentional community to be obtainable and applicable for anyone, anywhere, who was interested in and inspired by it, no matter the season or status of their life. I needed deep connection to people in these very specific ways to not just be limited to the single years of one's twenties, as I was quickly making my way out of mine. I needed Jonathan to have said that with a little bit of creative brainstorming and selflessness, another world was viable and willed for everyone in this very way.

Or at least anyone. At least that.

Because what would I find on the other side of this basket's deconstruction in which I had now placed all my eggs? Or rather, who would I find? Who would I find myself to be when the stability and foundation of the innkeeper began to rock?

7

Exposed Humanity

The Robber as Me

Regret is what you're feeling, sitting on your haunches in the dirt, jolting yourself across the ground with your heels until your back has slammed against the bark of the nearest tree.

Regret—that feeling you've worked so hard, for all of your life, to avoid. You begin to crawl up the surface of the tree with your spine, palms pressing down. Shoving a cloth into your mouth, you scream and sob out mucus into the soil and feel as if every good intention of yours was shedding right on off of you. Here it is: you're falling apart. It's finally here.

Take it back. Make it go away—this human, faulted, bad, bad side of you.

Erase it. Correct it and overcorrect it quickly.

You can't run far enough to get his moans out of your ears—the man that you were wrong about, the man that you all but destroyed, the man now caked with sand and blood who crossed your well-meaning path at the wrong damn time.

Will he live, you don't know—can't know—in your running. Will he live to tell the tale of your malformed soul? Will he live to heal from the cuts that you caused, replace the things that you stole, thrive again in a world where you are just as capable as the next guy of trampling the very life that God granted? You don't know. You can't know in your running.

Run, run, run, and remake yourself. Run, and rephrase, and get ahead of your own vulnerability.

Run with your life made up of all that you took, when you knew (and when you didn't) what you were taking.

Bloody Hands

"AND THIS IS WHAT the artist knows: the opposite of war is not peace, it is creativity . . ." James's melodic voice echoed through the Yellow House living room as he moved his arms theatrically and talked about activism and faith.

He joined us for morning prayer one week on a visit home before his move from California to New York. He added spirit, and wisdom, and—as a black man—pigment to our circle. His energy was contagious, and we'd talk for hours and hours after the coffee pot had long since announced it would be clocking out of morning duties.

Not having met when we were residents of the same city, we'd gush over how our paths, our experiences, and our faith-grappling were finding similar footing in different states and cultures. We'd talk theology and riff off of our different perspectives. He was a young African American living in the Northeast theater world, reading James Baldwin, Rob Bell, James Cone, and Rachel Held Evans. I was a young white woman living in the Bible Belt who had an extra copy of Claiborne and company's *Common Prayer: A Liturgy for Ordinary Radicals* and who was overtly insistent on showing him how all of his desires for the world and the church would fit nicely into the confines of what we had found in intentional community.

"But they don't, fully. Not yet." he insisted to me—now far too fascinated with him to be indignant.

"These expressions of Emergent faith are good because they reimagine a different way of being together," he paced as he talked. "They are versions of Christianity that undercut the system as if that system had no power over it. They reimagine a different way of being without having to go into that system. They reimagine success in America without it having to pertain to ladder-climbing and power-holding, and there's hope there. But I don't know that the conversations being had are on behalf of all people and the plights that they're actually dealing with."

My spirit put its hands up in an effort to cover the cracks in my ideology that were forming as he spoke. Again, I wanted so badly to have arrived at the answer to the seeker's question; and James was suggesting that we were in fact not quite there.

"Most rooms in which I sit where folks discuss how the church is changing now are made up of all white audiences talking about why millennials are leaving the faith—which is a white folk issue," he said. "White churches are *in* communities, and white people are leaving them. The black church is *of* a community. It became the place where people could exist and connect in ways that they were being disallowed to do in public spaces. How do you leave something that is a part of you even if you haven't 'attended' for years? The black community is dealing with other issues and this new era of Christianity will have to land at a place that includes them too."

Twenty-somethings leaving a church that wasn't getting to the heart of what it meant to *really* follow Jesus was not the pressing issue of Black America, James was suggesting; not the same way that it was for white people and for me. I admitted that I didn't understand, that I couldn't even wrap my mind around what would be the issue if not that.

Meanwhile, a constant and swelling social media feed from Ferguson, Missouri's month-old tragedy was suggesting that Michael Brown's murder would indeed be exposing a whole undercurrent of racism in our country that the white generations before us had insisted was long gone. And I'd believed it. All that would follow in our country would prove James to be right and me to be oblivious.

"Until the intellectualism of these theologies meets the streets of Ferguson, until the church can speak to real oppression, until they can hold the black trans woman's experience, we are not yet there. Whatever belief system comes out of all of this must support all people."

And mine didn't? And mine didn't, he'd all but said.

And mine didn't . . .

Which felt like it meant that I didn't—support all people, that is.

Which meant that maybe I was a part of the problem, or at least I might be adding to it. And in one moment, I blinked and went from glancing around the room of the inn's kitchen to standing in the dense woods by the road, blood on my hands.

White Folks

I don't even remember her name, or why she was there, or what group she'd accompanied on that big tour bus arranged monthly by our parent organization. But I vividly remember the feeling of wanting her out of my house.

She'd come through the squeaky screen door with the rest of her church's leadership, encircling our after-school program with their nice clothes and smells. We were functioning just fine—the teens, the interns, and me—in our now normal routine of disciplinary name marking, activity engaging, and chicken pot pie plating. They'd come to see a piece of the city and God's kingdom that they'd not known much about before. And now, at this point in my life, I felt like I was on the other side of the white-Christian-savior-complex, being observed instead of observing. The encouragement from our bosses suggested that we were to gain their involvement; however, the energy and hoop-jumping communicated that we wanted their money like all nonprofits wanted money so badly after the Great Recession.

"Tell me how this program has changed your life," she said right out of the gate, exposing every stark-white tooth of hers with an eager smile.

My kids and interns shot nervous looks around the crowded room.

"You know, like how your grades have gotten better or how maybe it's keeping you off of the streets?" She needed them to woo her with redemption that merited her tithe.

I cringed because it wasn't keeping them off of the streets, not really. The truth was that Dee had been kicked out for the rest of the semester because he'd stolen both my bike and Luke's and then called me a bitch on his way off our lawn. The truth was that Cameron was repeating the ninth grade again because his mama was God knows where, and his great uncle had cut his hair in the middle of the night while drunk, and he couldn't get enough sleep or enough food to study.

The truth was that I had stopped following most of them on social media because I was so tired of seeing pictures from their environments that made me feel less than safe. The truth was that some were doing so well with their grades and good behavior, but I knew that they were doing that before we came and would probably be doing it after we left.

The truth was, for two hours an afternoon, we were a small haven with a few expectations that made kids feel a little bit supported. We were a place that insisted they be the kids, and we be the adults, and they get seconds on food that they didn't have to prepare. And that was often hard to quantify for a donor. Its vital importance for all of us was hard to explain to someone who needed to know that their giving was changing the actual outcomes of statistically recordable teenagers' lives.

But there she was, talking to them like they were her project, exposing in me that they had very much been mine. Looking at her looking like me, I recognized the need for a good story to report back to a group whose culture was the same as hers.

Prove how you're changing, was the attitude. I wondered how James would shudder if he heard this; what he'd say to his black brothers and sisters once the lady left. What would he say to me?

I wanted to tell her that on more days than not, the one who was changing was me. The one that could be changing was her, if she'd listen, and sit, and not just drop in for a few minutes on a Thursday. So mad at her because I was so mad at me and my shared sentiments that had first brought me into that place, I turned to the kids after the group left and apologized for their coming.

"That's just white folks, Ms. B," a boy said with a smile. "Maybe we'll get a new basketball goal out of it." I got quiet at the thought of this dance, wondering what my do-gooder presence had robbed them of; wondering what dignity, and honesty, and comfort that I, the thief in all the history I represented and preserved, had stolen.

Dani came in with her leather bag of materials every Wednesday when I'd outsource our lessons. She was black, and bold, and a force of drive. She had to learn nothing about the kids, their culture, their language and background to connect. She was mighty successful, inspirational, and took no crap.

"I know this is what you do with your homeboys," she'd say. "And to be honest, it's also what I do with mine. But you're going to have to learn how to make it in this world and what's expected of you. Adopt the dialect and the rules of the white middle class so that you will be hired someday, and break the cycles of your family, and not get arrested. Whatever you do, when you are walking out here on these sidewalks and a cop turns on his lights, don't run. Stay calm. Call me."

As she preached, I wondered what hoops I'd been asking them to jump through with my skin and my reluctance to let them be more of who they were while on the property. Dani made me ask if I was the person for that position, or if I was just another white face setting standards that were under-informed. She made me think about my close community in the neighborhood, and how the people I was still sharing my living room with continued to be all people who looked and talked just like me. They'd simply moved into my neighborhood so that I could call them my neighbors.

Dani made me ask questions about gentrification and wonder if it had to do only with big developers or if it also pertained to how we lived our lives on our blocks. Our neighborhood association's online page had few poor, black and brown folks represented; our block parties had few white. I was hopping between both circles wanting violence to subside and wanting to not be the infiltrating churchgoer there to save the day or there to call the cops every time things got loud.

The clear lines were getting blurry as I wondered if we had even made one, true, outside-of-an-agenda friendship with a local neighbor during our entire tenure.

"Her family doesn't want her to give her child up for adoption," I shook my head in front of Dani while getting her up to speed about the pregnant fifteen-year-old in our program.

"Of course they don't, Britney," she said, muting my rambling and conjuring within me a dread about whether or not I had missed something huge.

"It isn't that simple. It isn't your culture, and it isn't that simple."

Walking with a Birth Mother

I'd asked Reagan a couple of months before, privately in my home office, if she could be pregnant. Her tall, tiny body had begun to bulge egg-like from her abdomen, and neighbors were talking.

"There's no way, Mrs. B," she assured me time and time again.

One afternoon during a volleyball game with some kids from our street, I watched her strenuously reach for a ball bolting her way. And a feeling sunk in my gut—she was pregnant and didn't know it, or didn't want to know it, or didn't want me to know it. That evening, we agreed that she would take an at-home test. And I sat watching her color shapes with crayons while the two pink lines surfaced.

Over the next few months, I learned more about the layers of "the system" as her adult sidekick while she navigated her third trimester and I navigated SNAPS forms. I learned that the phrase "work the system" easily dissolved with any time spent in the complicated, time-consuming, shame-piling, expensive run-around that was existing as poor. And I learned that my long-held-to, over-romanticized idealism for adoption could be in actuality a much sadder and more complex reality than what I had once daydreamed about. I was walking with a birth mother who would put a face with the other side of surrender papers. And that helped me to painfully see.

Since my church-employed years of adoption conferences, since the orphanages in Kenya and Haiti, I'd wanted a multi-racial family to give babies who didn't have families a place to enfold. I wanted to ease hurt and loneliness. I wanted to honor the theology of God's adoption made manifested among us. I had looked forward to it for years. And in some moments, I had built it up to be one of the most honorable acts that my husband and I could do together for the "least of this world," outside of living as New Monastics in our inner-city environment.

So when Reagan (whose baby, she'd been told by doctors, was too far developed for the abortion she'd desired) sat at my kitchen table and announced that she would not be single parenting, I was almost (and too quickly) giddy for the possibilities. Luke and I knew that this was not our child, as keeping the baby would mean losing the mom who now requested closed adoption. But we knew that it would be someone's child. And the baby would get a better chance. And the mom could finish school. And they would both have an opportunity to break some fairly predictable cycles.

Adoption was the answer. Adoption was the better story that I formed in my head like the lady had formed in hers when she toured our after-school program that day. Adoption, and the New Monastic lifestyle that had gotten us to adoption's door, were the best choices. I expected relief for everyone involved.

But what I didn't expect was the sadness. God, I didn't expect the sadness . . .

I didn't expect the neighborhood to fight so hard against her decision, for adoption to be such a daunting word.

I didn't expect Dani's face to drop when I told her what Reagan had decided to do.

I didn't expect her to be accused of unloving choices. I didn't expect those in her circle to support her dropping out of school rather than having another (probably white) family raise her child.

I didn't expect there to be so much anxiety about what negative narratives that black babies being raised in white homes might sustain about the black community.

I didn't expect Reagan's depression.

I didn't expect her to be torn between so many different voices. I didn't expect to learn that mine was one of the loudest, robbing her of peace about becoming *mama*.

I didn't expect her to feel hopeless, and helpless, and without resources.

I didn't expect her to shut down.

Feeling wildly under-qualified myself, I moved ahead with her adoption appointments (per her soft-spoken agreements), reluctantly reminding Reagan every step of the way that we could stop it all whenever she wanted. I did not realize the very power of insinuation that was me just being there with my obvious preferences.

But she'd nod, "No let's keep going," though (I'd later find out) her heart was beginning to love the little heartbeat inside of her, though she agreed with the accusations of her community, though she was spiraling into a dark place of passivity that one might expect of a fifteen-year-old whose entire, under-supported world was spinning on its head.

We considered bringing them both under our roof, however Reagan's mother had told her that she would neither allow her to live elsewhere nor would she assist her with the child should it be raised in their home. She'd heard mention of common words like Stamps and Medicaid, but even if rearing the baby in her mom's house was the chosen option, I was intensely aware of my inability to instruct her in the ways of social services without the help of someone more familiar.

She wanted to finish school and go to college. She wanted to be a kid going to parties. She wanted to eat fast food, and earn money babysitting, and go to her new boyfriend's house. She wanted to live at home. And now she wanted to keep her child.

I would never know the impossible, unfair weight of it all until I too would feel my child's first kick within me some two years later. And there I was, eager for the rehoming of another woman's flesh and blood. I cannot help but sob when I think about it.

We had made it all the way through to the family-choosing level of the adoption process with every rung to get there being painfully full of twists. But after the meeting, where she was presented profiles of families from which to choose, Reagan mustered up enough resolve in her hopeless and depressed state to tell me, "I want to raise my baby."

"Ok," I finally answered before we drove home in silence.

I canceled her agency appointments.

I planned a baby shower.

I called an organization that was willing to walk her through the piles of aid papers.

And I celebrated them both, mama and child, beneath three tons of grief and apprehension.

A few months after delivery, both mama and baby were surviving. Reagan had entered junior year with the crib and diapers she needed to function. And they were doing what it took to be a family. In the eleventh hour, her mom began to come around, though lines of communication remained rough. Interns would coordinate doctors' appointments as Reagan and I would tackle the embarrassing first rounds of WIC purchases together. We'd sit beside her in the lobbies and living rooms where she'd fill out hours of paperwork. And she'd end up making it in a way that I had not wanted to define "making it": in school, and in a crowded home, and with the baby who was being fed by the young, poor mother who wanted to keep her.

What had been laid bare in my own soul was my simple and misplaced understanding of and desire for how a community of people not my own was supposed to conduct itself. Something like adoption (what I had concluded as the answer) could be powerful, and good, and hopeful. But it was not perfect. And it was, at least in this case, drenched in loss.

Afterward, I could not put the idea of it on my polished shelves, beside a picture of our multi-colored family and our intentional community, and look upon it with pride, honor, and a pat on my own damn back. I had to, after this, approach adoption with fear and trembling, seeing the grief and injustices that had led to the pain and bravery that a birth mother like Reagan (who'd been left in the dust of systems from which I benefited) could experience. I had long embraced the chasm of loss that adoption's bridge could cross, but now I was obligated to ask what other bridges was I not considering, prioritizing, investing in, and defending.

Which ones was I burning: bridges like staring longer and more honestly at the racism and poverty that held the reins of Reagan's circumstances; bridges like supporting whole families and investing in resources for young mothers; bridges that were hairy, and hard, and not as glorified as adoption had become in my head and in what seemed to be our white, modern, evangelical Christian culture.

Until I saw the sadness that adoption could bring about, I did not know its power to heal and to wound. I did not know that my path (before Reagan) was leading me to a scenario that lacked great lamentations, humility, and repentance warranted for a world where babies are not being raised by the mothers who conceive them.

I did not know how warped was my eagerness to volunteer to parent the product of the inequalities I was perpetuating and from which I was profiting.

Piling

Over the next few months, I would encounter more under-informed, judgmental, and scared versions of myself than I knew what to do with. We traveled to Nogales, Arizona for an Immigration Immersion experience, only for me come face to face with the stigmas and misinformation that I didn't realize I held regarding migrants and the Hispanic community. I listened to stories of war and famine from which families would escape, and wondered what I might do if my own country were ever to experience such a plight. What would I do if no other country would let us in? How many years had I not considered this possibility? How many years had I not cared to hear something different than what I assumed?

When Alton Sterling was murdered in Baton Rouge and a Black Lives Matter march was organized in front of our courthouse four hours away, I sat at home in my recliner, too terrified to join with a community so susceptible to being shot. I'd done the same when the LGBT community and those who love them gathered at the same courthouse after Omar Mateen killed forty-nine people in Orlando.

I wondered those nights, for hours of tortured consideration, what cause would feel big enough to make me decidedly willing to risk being killed by some zealous priest-turned-monster in my own town, where everyone is able to carry their anger and their weapons of war with them wherever they go.

What plight would help me to know what the martyrs of the revolutions and the storytelling survivors knew? What the marchers at Selma, and the protesters at death row, and the Christian Peacemaker Teams in the Middle East knew? Quickly, shatteringly, I was getting a front row seat in finding out who I would have been in all the scenarios in history that seemed to really matter.

Sitting in my living room those evenings, as videos circulated of lit candles being held by preachers with their toddlers on their shoulders in our downtown streets, I screamed into a pillow about how very sorry I was for being so terrified and weak. I was so sorry that many have to live much of their lives that much more terrified as people in the world rage about in their own fear of what they represent for them.

I ached desperately for the bravery that my black and gay neighbors demonstrated just by existing as themselves. I longed for a time when all (the shooter, the victim, the scared and straight friend) didn't have to be so incredibly fearful.

What had come out in the wash of a world under threat was my own revealed and ugly self-preservation.

As it turned out, I had a limit to what I would risk and where I would go, for whom I would stand, and march, and light candles; for whom I would live and die.

As it turned out, I was no better than the twisted sympathizers, and stagnant couch-sitters, and barbaric robbers of my worst nightmares.

Belief had been malleable, but now action was optional. And I was indeed wretched when I wanted to be so very good. It was turning out that I was a warped soul in a world where people like Dani, and Reagan, and Ethan deserved for me to be better than the detestable thief that I could no longer unsee myself as being.

Out

When Ethan moved into our intentional community house the year after he finished college, he lit up the whole property with his music and his searching mind. More delightful energy and intuitive ideas could be found in one hour with him than in a week with most others, and I fell in love with his personality so quickly.

He'd spent the summer in Costa Rica hiking trails and drinking coconut milk. I couldn't have loved more the Caribbean background of his Skype interview to get into our program. He came to Highland with a box of beautiful sea-foam and ruby mugs that he'd thrown on his own pottery wheel. He was a student of agriculture with insight into the planting seasons, the good bugs, and the dead leaves needed for enriched soil.

His wild hair would fly about his face as he'd bounce up and down on that old blue recliner he'd dragged into our living room from his dorm. He was a good friend, a dedicated community member, a set of strong lungs that brought music back into our common space after a good while of it having been mostly gone.

Halfway through our ministry's fifth year, Ethan came out in a way that felt similar to my conversation with Mary, except with more timbre in his voice. He came out first to us as the house's leadership and then quickly to its residents as an imposed and clumsy condition of inexperienced, covenantal living. His personal process—rushed by my naive insistence that the common life meant for all things to be shared at all times—surfaced a spectrum of belief within the program. And talk of right and wrong inched its way into hushed corners of porches and kitchens.

"I don't know how to guide him," I confessed to a progressive pastor friend whom I assumed to be without hesitation or question regarding Ethan's path as good and designed.

"Britney," he paused for a while, looking at the floor. "When it's all said and done, we could be wrong. But I'm going to err on the side of love and room-making to give people the space to hear God themselves. You don't need to guide him. You need to listen."

I needed to hear this pastor's convictions mixed with half-an-ounce of uncertainty to be able to embrace that I still had some as well. The words "we could be wrong, and yet . . ." freed me to not have it all together on the hearing side of another's process.

Ethan spent the rest of the year exploring the depths of his faith and sexuality's intersection while we listened, and prayed, and gardened the squash, and sang the hymns. As he told stories of perpetual pain and spotty peace, as I held his folded body while he wept for a relationship with his mom and talked about all those years that he wished to be nothing more than dead, as we shared the theorizing, the learning, the guessing, the redirecting, we became bound.

I learned to respect Ethan's path as sacredly and utterly not my own. And yet we were walking it together: his gift to me.

A year into our friendship, any time I was remotely tempted to prioritize the rule-keeping and the answer-preserving above the room-making and wound-healing, I'd think about Ethan and how much poorer my life would be without having him—all of him—as a part of it. I'd think about the music, the service, the encouragement, the recipes, the bravery, the conversations, the family, the collaboration, his spirituality, his sexuality, the space for my gifts and weaknesses, and the willingness to embrace the wonder. And I'd cry because I knew that I almost missed out.

I'd cry as I'd think about the larger church body, and I'd ask what we were missing with our gatekeeping and with our worry.

I'd cry as I'd think back on every single person who had likely felt, over the last decade, that my distance, voice, silence, or rebuttals for a subject that I truly could not even begin to understand had made them feel less loved by God, welcomed by community, and embraced as and for every bit of who they'd be bringing to how we were growing.

And this was the fear that now haunted me: *How many gay people had I wounded? How many black and brown? How many poor, with the zeal of my faith? How many grieving, with my insistence for fast redemption? How many had I robbed?*

And was there swift redirection to still be had? Could I apologize, or clarify, or become open and affirming enough to make up for the fact that I still wondered if any classmates of mine were out there in the world weeping with their folded bodies into someone's lap, wishing rather for death than to live a life of what I once suggested was the decidedly wrong kind of love, showing up at the courthouse and looking around only to never see more people like me.

Me: the robber hiding in the bushes of my own sin against who knows how many wounded children of a loving God.

Undoing

Meanwhile, as I was standing at the center of a tug-of-war between my idealism and my shame, our community house was being groomed for replication by our supervisors even in and amongst funding struggles. I could not help but lose sleep over whether or not it was even a good thing to have, much less to clone, much less to clone at a time when finances for our larger organization were so month to month (if that).

At the end of each year, we would sit pouring over the House Covenant, marking with red ink all the guidelines that needed increased specificity—raising the bar higher and higher regarding substances, sexual ethics, relationships among housemates, and demands for how conflict would, *without exceptions*, be handled. Our once fairly short list of suggestions had grown to be a multi-pages document in our attempts to control the house, and we were still experiencing hiding, and lying, and line-crossing in close quarters that seemed to always be spreading like wildfire. I'd wonder if we were just becoming priests again with a new vernacular. I'd wonder if a house full of single college grads was the right season of life on which to place such expectations. I'd wonder, increasingly, if it was even our place to do so. I'd wonder if we'd ever get the mind-space to figure it out with how often we were stressing about possibly not getting paid and performing for donors who might remedy such a dilemma.

There was a method to the fundraising. Typically, an older, white man in professional business-wear accompanying one of our employers would step over the threshold. Towards the end of our community's life, no rehearsal was needed. We had perfected a system for donor-dances: explain how we were making leaders, share how we were growing family and purpose in a generation that can get lost in its own selfish living, demonstrate how we were creating avenues for dedicated service and experiences that would make for better wives, neighbors, teachers, and voters.

Our program staff would share about our curriculum and our (wary) ideas for expanding and replicating. We would talk about franchising into four more neighborhoods, three more cities, at least one more country alongside our parent organization. Our interns would share about their aimless, friendless existences before. They'd tell about finding a place to process losing parents, or having been abused, or having lost their faith. There was such undeniable fruit dropping off of the branches for a potential donor to observe. And we could see it too, despite all the fires that we were steadily putting out.

The visitors would leave to go off and consider us for check-writing. We'd stay to grieve who we were becoming. I'd stay to grieve how I was possibly selling the soul of our desired lifestyle for a "bigger and best" version of something of which I was growing quite skeptical.

Missing, still, was an organic base of community to which the internship could be attached. By now, we had met people from about a dozen intentional and New Monastic communities who had established internships (or novice programs) for people to come, see, learn, serve, and then maybe even to stay. But we had no stability, despite how often we taught about it; no net for catching those who were rotating out of the program's two years; no covenanted body of people into which one might enfold outside of the controlled environment that we had so meticulously crafted and recrafted. Typically, internships offer a small window into a more established lifestyle or employment. Yet, our internship was the most established place that one could get in our attempts at living intentionally.

Our last December in the house, we traveled the ten-hour drive from Shreveport to Clarence Jordan's Koinonia Farms in Americus, Georgia. There, we sorted nuts for one of the community's income-bringing businesses, prayed liturgy in their on-site chapel with their covenanted members and summer interns, learned of the place's reconciling history and the familiar rhythm of pruning and growing, withering and changing.

Americus confirmed that communal existence brought with it an unavoidable fluidity that could mean that even among the existence of promises and talk of commitment, things were always being reshaped. People were always leaving, and slow-growth and perpetual modifications would always be a part of the New Monastic life. But what it also confirmed for me was that we did not personally have the foundation that would hold through the changes that could be expected for a community of that nature. We were still just a program of white young adults:

a transitional, temporary experience calling itself a body of lon-
gevity, stability, and inclusion.

"Is there a place in your community for someone like me,"
the woman in her thirties wearing the mandatory hair net and
gloves asked while we packaged the pecans. "I'm a furniture
builder, artist, skeptic. I've been here all summer, and am looking
for my next step."

I told her yes, because I wanted it to be the truth. I wanted so
badly to not be grappling deeply with who we were and what we
were and weren't creating.

*Yes, one could move two states away, find a rent house in High-
land, and have people to pray and garden with daily. Yes, there would
be folks there for the long haul. Yes, we had carved out a rhythm of
life in the inner city for spiritual exploration, contemplation, and
shared possessions that could enfold the middle-aged single, the
runaway teen, the family-of-four, or the old and poor and brown
and rich. No, we weren't the robbers or the priests. Yes, we were the
Samaritans and innkeepers (and sometimes still the seekers). Yes,* is
what I wanted to be true.

But it wasn't. The truth was, had she moved, she would have
been quite alone.

There was no place for her here, not an established one at
least; and I am so grateful that she never shifted her entire life to
find out what I was ignoring. There was only an internship that
was trying to multiply with pressures from its funders while chaos
frequently broke out within its walls—a concept getting bigger
and unrulier while I craved so deeply for it to get smaller and
truer. She would have found what everyone living outside of our
program or who eventually left it did find: a living room to pray in
periodically and a group of people who loved the idea of it being
so much more than that.

*What had it all become? Where were our forever people, our
forever system, forever way? Why were we in charge of so much and
so little? How had we become the wounders and the wanderers when
we had relocated to be the bandagers and the housers?*

Money and pitches for bigger programs for more money were making things extra complicated externally as things grew more difficult internally. We missed taking communion, so we tried to make a house church. We wanted financial freedom, so we tried to develop an income-bringing retreat plan. We needed more interns, so we printed more fliers, visited more services, did more dances. We wanted less conflict and fewer secrets, so we edited and reedited more covenants again and again and again. We ate our words, and shifted our gears, and added and added and fixed while longing for that contemplative, simple life that seemed to never quite be within reach despite the energy and sanity sacrificed at the altar of steady alterations.

All the while, we were trying to recreate the refining environment of peer-level confession and adventure; and paying our bills and running the day-to-day level of things; and longing for a life that was doing less damage in the world, that was less scared, less fake, and more good.

And then, an unforeseen thing happened. The doing (and doing good, doing now, and doing well before being discovered for doing bad) led to the undoing.

The doing, so very ironically, led to the undoing, after all.

8

The Last Closed Door

The Wounded

Where are you?
What is this place?
What all . . . just happened?

The thoughts are circling, searching for a landing strip, while you attempt to break open your eyelids. With one swollen shut and the other feeling as if it is holding a migraine unto itself, you're able to catch only a small glimpse of your surroundings. Briefly. The sunlight, it is so oppressive now.

You're remembering, but what? You trusted someone. But who? A stranger? A friend? A road? Yourself?

It all happened so fast, and now you're here, on the ground, fading. You attempt to roll your hips to roll the rest of your body anywhere, but nothing moves except for the synapses firing off, yelling about everything that is broken inside of you. All of a sudden, you feel as exposed and crippled as you are—as you've never been before.

Weak.
Limited.
Vulnerable.

Wounded.

Unequipped to recover and run if the forces were to return. And they may—you know this.

Your tear ducts overflow with waters so real and so deep that they shift not a muscle on your face. "Hopeless," is the only word you can muster, and as you speak it into existence a surge of truth runs through your being. You are—God help us all—hopeless.

You are in so much need.

You are desperate for a person to cross your path though you haven't the lung capacity to call out for one.

You are done for.

You are done.

You are finally, tragically, human.

Labor

AT 3 A.M., LUKE and I awakened abruptly to the sound of our neighbor's drunk boyfriend singing country songs into the dark from the back of their screened-in porch, which sat a mere ten feet from our pillows. We greeted each other—having been thrown out of slumber—with grumpy groans and laughter.

"Good morning, Highland." We rolled our eyes as I swung my five-days-overdue belly into the sky and planted swollen feet the size of throw pillows onto our floor. In the thick of our growing number of things to resolve, we'd found out that we were going to have a son.

Drowsily, and with much effort, I made it to the bathroom where I lived most of the third trimester.

"Luke. I think my water just broke?" I cackled toward the bedroom, "The baby must have heard that God-awful singing."

I'd packed all the necessities for the hospital: a newborn outfit, snacks for Luke, our birth plan, my limping-but-breathing invincibility. I'd hoped so deeply to be able to labor at home for 90 percent of the experience and to show up at the hospital for a few simple pushes and a positive testimony toward swift, un-medicated, empowering childbirth. I white-knuckled only a few basic ideals that seemed fair enough to value: a natural birth, a breastfed baby, and a reality of parenthood that could fit neatly into the life of community and faith work that I'd been so carefully controlling, chasing, and reworking.

Motherhood was another woman's journey leading all the way up until my pregnancy (and a bit after). That calling into nurture, bodily fluids, and sleeplessness appeared little more than limiting, identity-stripping, and haggard compared to my thoughts about changing the world. It looked like the siren that drew otherwise social adults into the rocky cliffs of isolation; a nail in the coffin of the American dream's opposite that I'd worked so diligently to discover and develop.

Being formerly, rarely ever compelled to even acknowledge a baby in the arms of another adult to whom I'd be speaking, I recognized few deep yearnings (and even less confidences) within myself as *mama*. But I knew family. And I knew we wanted family. And I knew the power of having a family whose walls could be made wider.

We decided to try for pregnancy simply because our stars of feeling "right enough" had aligned. Luke and I both felt brave and willing simultaneously, which is maybe as big of a miracle as pregnancy itself. The news of our soon-to-be-son was met with grand celebration by our family and friends and those with whom we prayed every morning across the street. I feared not that he would be raised by anything other than a village of ever-present, ever-close community throughout his upbringing.

He would be born into a body of people dedicated to living in proximity to one another, to sharing their lawn mowers, to making covenants. He would learn to ride his bike on streets where not all of the kids looked, talked, and ate like him. He would run around the halls of the second floor in that old yellow house on Sunday mornings if we could ever figure out what church in that place, in that time, looked like.

He'd learn connectedness, belonging, garden growth, vows of friendship and of stability as important as any others. He'd learn about God's unconditional love for all people, practical application of good news, the art of neighboring. He would tuck seamlessly into our well-built rhythm of 8 a.m. liturgy, late night heart-to-hearts, marches at the parks to stand with love and protest violence.

I looked forward, with few other expectations, to parenthood as I had looked forward to many other uncharted seasons: with a determination to live it out in such a way that it could be a good example and a great story of full and faithful life.

Our boy came earth-side around eight on a Thursday evening after forty-one hours of intense, traumatizing labor. I held his bafflingly calm body bundled over the fresh and medicated laceration of my abdomen and wondered when he might feel like mine. *Would he feel like mine?*

The weeks following were no healing balm to the wound that was recognizing my body's own barriers. With every pediatric appointment, every weigh-in that indicated that the taxing and mysterious transaction of milk was not occurring like it needed to be occurring, as my plump baby began to look like a shrinking, cartoon bat and I still could not lift myself off of a chair without deep pain and sadness, I felt my light dimming. The long-anticipated, spotty sleep was compounded greatly by the aching infant whimpers droning on and on after feedings, further confirming our fears and multiplying our questions. *Could I give him what he needed?*

I had fewer natural instincts than I knew were possible as his caregiver, spending hours each week on the phone with pediatricians and our parents. And, as I'd never before experienced, I could now not escape my own terrible weaknesses. I could not escape all that was causing me a great deal of fear and emotional anguish.

We made do how we needed to. We finally introduced some formula; we relied heavily on our parents; we let people assist us with food, cleaning, and listening weeks after what so many births often elicit.

Our baby was calm and peaceful; I knew from the monitors at the hospital that he would also be resilient. His infancy was quickly becoming my teacher and my warden, an usher of my soul into the fires that would make me a different person, eventually. His almond eyes would blink past the folds of his swaddle, focused as if he was made to connect. I wanted so desperately to be better for him—physically, mentally, emotionally better—like I'd wanted to be better for Dani, and Raegan, and Ethan, and about eight different cultures and communities. But my will was waning with this new experience vigorously uncovering all my innate incapability.

My phone alarm would stir us out of our naps in time for the next feeding. I would wake directly into a shortness of breath and an unshakeable amount of doom that accompanied the every-two-hour experience of facing my own agony (agony necessary to wade for the nourishment of my child, an agony that was producing very little detectably in return, an agony that was slowly sucking away my concept of reality).

All that was left was hard. The teas, the cookies, the pumps, and the consultations to increase breastmilk were proving to be powerless against my stubborn supply (or lack thereof). Nursing was causing blisters, and blood, and infections for which I hadn't prepared in the least. I'd trace the raised tissue left from my cesarean and remember how no ideal, or dedication, or mantra, or determination for a natural and limitless experience could have changed the hard with which we were now left. Depression and anxiety, though they didn't have names at the time, moved into my house alongside relentless mother-love, making all things unsettled—not seamlessly grafted-in as I'd expected. Hard had become our new life.

We were in new territory where it was growing more and more difficult to not be riddled with every negative emotion, let alone to get across the street for morning prayer. Without being able to even so much as nod toward my typically agile capacity to shift and include whatever community and purpose meant at the time, my spirit was—as if in the dark of the night—turned off.

It was shut down like field lights after a Friday night game, except this time, before the players could realize that the clock was up.

And the crashes ensued.

Like the suffering that had thwarted the security, the harm that had thwarted the help, the misconduct that had thwarted the missions of all my past attempts at finding the way that one should be walking, the path of right journey began to deconstruct itself yet again—only this time through the distanced lens of maternity leave. Motherhood, and the all-hands-on-deckness of our lives and the impossibly big love swelling in our hearts, had become a distinct and unarguable rubric for what really mattered. And I had not prepared.

Nothing Has Changed

The buzz of my cell phone pestered us out of deep, insatiable sleep as the call pressed through from our interns who obviously did not know what they faced by stirring a new-mom whose child was not screaming. They'd said a woman had been thrown out of a moving truck by an abusive lover, right between our houses. Hot tea was steeping across the road as the residents worked to decipher her slurring words that seemed to be indicating that she did not, no matter what, want to call the cops. I asked for a few minutes to find my pants, shoved the baby monitor into Luke's side, and trudged through our yard.

It was "radical hospitality to the stranger" month in our intentional community internship, which was unfortunate timing for our new and newly inhospitable lives. The housemates scurried about the home finding blankets and Band-Aids while I called 911 to deal with the problem that I needed resolved quickly. They whispered between each other about the miracle of having prayed for a chance to say yes to a knock on the door as if it were Christ himself. I watched the weeping woman, knowing I would not, could not, offer her a bed of ours with our new child one hall down and her very mad boyfriend somewhere out in the world.

I pieced myself together in a way that I hoped still communicated that I was not scared, that I was still willing, that nothing had changed. Nothing had changed.

But the truth was that those twelve beautiful, hard marks of the New Monastic life were getting harder and harder to sustain (as I understood them). We had re-homed our shelter mutt because her hair on our pacifiers was making me homicidal. Her absence freed one ounce of energy to wash a bottle or a spoon when needed, but recycling, and contemplation, and even remotely keeping up with the injustices of the world (much less my posture toward and actions following them) seemed altogether impossible.

We packed away our time-swallowing cloth diapers and signed up for monthly disposable bundles. I felt the landfill breathing down my neck, calling me a fraud, waving goodbye to the person who knew better about God's good, green earth. Healthy and deep conflict, confrontation, and conversation were still bettering our little block's bunch, but they'd begun to zap our little family's already zapped days so entirely that I was losing words and the ability to be near people.

I was becoming depressed.

And I was starting to admit it: I was unable to make decisions, all of the sudden paralyzed by the thought of parties and travel. My feelings were numb, my chest cavity like a void. My hair was falling out, and I felt as if I were more hidden than I had ever been. I was in a pit with no rope and no voice, watching shadows pass by topside. My insides were unrecognizable. My outsides grew to be as well while our home and our surroundings surged with pressures.

Crime began to increase, it felt, inching closer and closer to our street in a way that it had not done in five years. Murders and cocaine rings would roll through the page of our online neighborhood watch, and the pop-pop-pops of gunshots that we'd normalized as background noise now felt like a more fearsome threat to our growing family.

It seemed that civic morale was decreasing as the disgusting and perilous political river roared on into everybody's living rooms. And throughout our city, stabbings, home invasions, and kids pulling guns out at stop signs flared on about and found their way into my chest as a new and constant companion: anxiety.

The night after friends of ours at a sister-house two neighborhoods over miraculously had their lives spared during a nonsensical drive-by whose bullets came within twelve inches of the husband's body, Luke and I discussed where we would take our son if shots ever sounded that close. The bathtub, it was decided, if we had the time. And in a way that I had not yet done since we'd moved onto Dalzell, I imagined my life elsewhere. My dedication to the long haul, for which I had faulted so many priests, Levites, Samaritans, innkeepers, and robbers for abandoning, was now entirely negotiable.

Meanwhile, our parent-organization continued on in its culture of perpetuating and expecting expansion. And, in some ways I think, why wouldn't it? Why wouldn't the organization also expect it of us, we who had seemed to know what we'd signed up for from the beginning? But the more talk happened about replication, infiltration into other places, teaching, recording, and (hope to the heavens) funding, the further it felt we were getting from that shared, grass-roots, monastery-style existence that I now needed (and needed to work) more than ever.

Hopeless

Our community considered separating from the larger organization, breaking away and breaking down in order to get smaller and smaller one more time. On top of everything else, we willingly entered into months of deliberation about how we might start new—unanchored, unfunded, but maybe truer to our calling that was simultaneously worth fighting for and now also unnervingly optional.

Daycare and diapers were unanticipatedly aggressive to our checking account. We had begun to tap into our small savings a little more every month. Though we shared much with our community and both worked two solid forty-plus hour jobs in the arts and nonprofits, it seemed we were barely treading water. With us having left the youth house and returned to the bungalow across from the interns in order to gain a bit more privacy with a child, our bills doubled just as our laundry did.

That fall, after using all of my sick days for the two dozen viruses that come with a baby's first year in childcare, after answering (or not answering) a hundred knocks with a hundred needs at our front door, after Luke and I lost all of the tools we'd accumulated in learning how to love each other well, after battling a now rampant anxiety and a burrowing depression that was gluing me to my couch on the weekends and evenings, after our counselor had all but begged us to make wider margins and better boundaries in our lives, after we had to cancel our appointments with her because we could no longer afford them, after the guilt of sharing the raising of my son with other women when I questioned the work that was keeping me from him—when I wasn't always certain that I'd even get a paycheck for it—after I admitted that we were still missing a peer-level community who could properly help us shoulder these burdens, after I saw my life for what it had become (conflicted, removed of options, compromised, and painful), after all of this, I found myself on the edge of our bed staring stoically at the broken doors of my armoire. And I mumbled—as if into an abyss—words that I had never, not one time in my life, said.

"I feel hopeless." And I meant it.

Had that even come out of my mouth? Did I make a sound, or just think it?

Luke reversed his forward stroll down our hallway with a folded load of laundry in hand. His eyes communicated that he was scared, though his voice remained steady.

"Hopeless?" he asked, worried.

Definitely . . . completely . . . hopeless.

I'd lost months of rest even after our baby had begun sleeping through the night, lying awake in bed relentlessly going over option after option of how we might be who we said were going to be all those years ago when we said we were going to be them. I tried to slow my breathing as I thought about how we might get the money, the hours, the capacity, and the community again (or for the first time or whatever). I brainstormed over and over how we could possibly break away, make it work, and still believe that it all remained to be so very important to us and to God, that it did more good than harm, that it was worth it.

My body was turning into a bulging vat of adrenaline. My heart and my routine were turning into that of a fierce and attached mama in love with her tiny, dependent child. I felt my whole existence—and my squirmy, precious boy whose eyelashes stuck together in triangles at bath time—imploring me to figure out a different reality with less brokenness, more stability, less stimuli, more peace. I *needed* to do this lest our spirits die and our whole ministry disintegrate, taking with it our values, our understanding of church, our people, our calling, our career, our neighbors, our work, our plights, and our friends.

I was on a fast track to melting right on into the earth, it felt, here when I was needed more than I'd ever been needed before; here when I now needed more than I'd ever needed before.

Lava

Then one night at eleven, with my body bent over, head between knees, I hunkered in our bathroom after months of torturous consideration. My ears felt so filled with stress that they could have very well been pouring hot lava straight from their canals and onto our unmopped tiles. I wondered if the veins in my torso would just pop into dark red confetti on the spot, if my breathing would just finally vanish, if I might have a heart attack the year before I turned thirty. My head was ringing. My hands were clenching. My eyes were shifting. My soul was begging. And then, it all stopped.

And I saw the rope-end. There it was. In the bathroom, two decades after I'd asked Jesus to show me the way to the biggest, best, and most meaningful life: there was the rope's end.

And as if dropping my very last card in a scattered pile of bad hands on the floor in slow motion, I looked up at my ghost-white face in our mirror, hands on the sink, sweating. And I allowed myself to fumble a question around my mouth which I had refused as an option for over a year—or five, or ten, or twenty years.

"What if it's all just over?"

The thought sent steady lines of tears pouring on to my shirt. I heaved in and out as a rush of air filled my lungs. I had considered endings plenty of times before, but only when next steps had already presented themselves, only when new paths, visions, purposes, and iterations of faith sat waiting for me on the other side. This was different. It was an ending that was not accompanied by a redirection. It was simply, and completely, *no more.*

It did not take twenty-four hours to discover that I was not the only one feeling this truth as the rest of the house's leadership and the counsel around us confirmed the still, small voice ushering us in the same direction. We needed stability and peace and to live within our means, it was decided. And so, as if someone else that I had loved so enormously had been diagnosed with a disease, we announced our closure and our community was given just a few months' worth of goodbyes left to exist.

My first baby. My values. My understanding of church. My people. My calling. My career. My ever shifting, but always persisting way, until then.

An onslaught of crippling grief and pure, raw peace filled me to the edges. And then I slept—finally slept—all night long in the wet, bloody, sunken dirt of the wounded, roadside man.

I was dying; or so it felt. And I didn't care.

Last Song

A spread of wholesale finger foods covered the sticky, white-tiled cabinet that we'd wiped 400 times for 200 events before. Filing in through the old, front door were the pastors who had taught us, the neighbors who had cooked for us, the musicians who had shared with us, the residents who had—over the years—cut pieces of their own lives right off and planted in the soil of that lot.

I suppose it's easier to explain why you're ending something intrinsically harmful or obviously ineffective. It was much harder to explain why we'd choose to kill something that was producing fruit when so much of what outweighed the fruit went unseen or remained so personal.

We tried our best through metaphors and long conversations over chips and salsa to articulate. We tried our best to communicate our great need for constancy and sustainability. We shared what we could about the expenses and finances, the weird lines made and crossed with money, the emotional depth of working with multiple young adults, the questions we had about all the rules we had made as the innkeepers-again-the-priests, the physical state of our old and precarious houses, the volatile nature of the neighborhood we'd chosen to live in and love, the questions about our own efforts and the good versus the harm, the nasty systems of the world that kept us in cowardice, and the changing of our life seasons and surrounding support. We had been wanting for energy and peace for so long that we could feel it in our teeth; so we were digging the grave ourselves, and singing dirges all the while.

We held a farewell concert and shared some of our favorite songs we'd written while trying to chase Jesus down a modern, monastic road. I tried to make eye contact with every beating, bleeding heart in the room during our last song, before the boxes got moved, before the Yellow House became 410 Dalzell once again.

And we chanted a song that I had written for our little group of people years before:

> We moved into a house, we could not afford
>
> And dropped all baggage down atop nail-ridden boards
>
> We thought it'd be easy, we thought it'd be fast
>
> We thought gray loneliness was a thing of the past
>
> We would rise in the spring, crash in the fall
>
> As our impulsive natures made fools of us all
>
> But it got us to leap, oh it taught us to fly
>
> And we prayed as we bled to land on the other side
>
> And we waited, oh how we waited

We waited, oh how we waited

But You came at the end of a rope that we didn't even know we were on

You gave us the courage to fight that we didn't even know was long gone

Your grace is what we met, we have no regret from jumping

Because you gave us family

We laid beds of stone and put our hands in the dirt

As we asked the body to reflect the good of the earth

We were stripped paper thin as we warred for desire

But we know what God does when God uses fire

And we waited, oh how we waited

We waited, oh how we waited

You came at the end of a rope that we didn't even know we were on

You gave us the courage to fight that we didn't even know was long gone

Your grace is what we met, we have no regret from jumping

Because you gave us family

And we march on, to the full life You declare

We march on, until we all are there

We march on, to the full life You declare

We march on, until we all are there.

It took six months for the sobbing to start. Six months for the existential dread to fully set in. Six months to find a new job that even remotely covered what my family needed and had any connection to what I thought might still be my interests (if I had any).

Six months for me to realize what I had lost. Six months for the questions to start churning relentlessly in my head about my identity, our community, and what our faith meant now. Six months for almost everyone in our group to finally move out of the neighborhood, leaving Luke and I to raise our son and lick our wounds. Six months for me to realize that nothing pronounced, nothing clear, nothing like community, nothing radical had fleshed out on the other side of our ending. All my life, when one door would close, another one had always been opened either by fate or the force of my own two hands. But now my fate felt damned, and my hands broken, and my doors, all shut.

Six months to see that nothing picked up where the other had left off. Six months to fully arrive at my soul's darkest night, which only felt like one thing: that it would be forever.

The End

An excerpt from my journal at the time:

> *I'm so mad at you*
>
> *for infusing me with desires*
>
> *for an impossible life.*
>
> *How dare you.*
>
> *I'm so mad at us*
>
> *for never getting to where we were going*
>
> *all that time we were going.*
>
> *What waste.*
>
> *I'm so mad at them,*
>
> *all of the fake-ass people who looked like me*
>
> *when I looked like them.*
>
> *All frauds.*

The priest, whose language no real person could understand,

The Levite, who was basically the priest wrapped in false kindness,

The Samaritan, who loved that she loved so damn well,

The robber, who reared her head in every soul I thought to be good, including my own,

The innkeeper, whose stable house was never, ever truly attainable,

And me.

God, I'm so mad at me,

and sad for me,

and tired of me,

and a stranger to me

and terrified for me

that there's no one else to be

in this story.

So, I guess this is just

. . . the end.

9

An Outstretched Hand

Both, All

You awaken to the drum of footsteps emitting through the bedrock that's directly under your pounding head. You should be dead by now. Are you dead right now?

You made peace with your demise hours ago, or so this is the timeframe that the migrated sun that's blistered your body would suggest. There's no time, or need, or energy to sort through all that got you here—only the last drop of will to yield to the pain. There is no one else to become, no tactics left to try, nowhere else to go but into the freeing, harrowing waters of surrender.

But then, a dirt-caked cloak bottom appears in your peripheral. You pay it no mind as no one's likely to stop, as no one has stopped all day. You've become a blind spot, background noise, someone able to be snuffed out of the picture of your own perception. Why would anyone else see you, much less pause? Unless, of course they are the ones who have come to make you pay. Come to handle the judgment hour you strived so hard for so long to dodge.

Come to kick dirt in the face of the one who got it wrong.

Come to remind you of all the ways you were unloving.
Overeager.
Self-obsessed.
Weak.
Unable to live the life that Jesus had once described.

They've come to make you pay for all of the ways that your need for control, your abuse of privilege, your missteps, failures, brokenness, blindness, and now exhaustion rippled through their world, knocking who knows how many off their feet; come to charge you for your pious passing, weak justifications, harmful help, do-good damage, failed attempts that missed the mark.

Like a beaten dog, your adrenaline pumps through your shoulders and before you know it, you're shaking your fingers toward the figure. "I'm sorry! I'm sorry! I'm so, so sorry!" you scream. Or, you try.

"I was wrong! I was wrong. Forgive me, and let me die!" Your voice cracks, your purple lips quiver at the thought of no one hearing your apology before the grave takes you whole. But then, the cloaked one's hand reaches yours, and the figure lowers itself to the ground beside you as the hood drops low to her shoulders. Her other hand sandwiches yours in something that feels like embrace.

You realize, as she uses her middle finger to tuck your damp and soiled hair behind your ear, that she . . . how is this possible . . . is you.

"You're ok," she says, you say, maternally and like a friend. "We're ok."

A long pause lets the world turn around you both while you attempt to sort what is real and what is not.

Finally, she speaks again. "I need you to know that I forgive you." The words are whispered, her esophagus gulping for a breath before her smiling eyes turn on like hydrants. "I forgive us."

Your hands are holding your hands in a grip so tightly that it chases the color away, and you push yourself up with your elbow like a kickstand, staring, scowling, unbelieving, and saved.

"I forgive us, and we can forgive them: all the neighbors who look like who we used to be and all the ones we haven't yet become."

*This is mercy. You feel it. You know it now because
you need it now.
This is what they meant when they talked about it all
along.
It is mercy.
And it's yours.*

Grieving

OUR SON RESTED, SWINGING in the only contraption that could
keep his reflux at bay while I colored mandalas with markers—a
tactic that my former counselor had said might get my breathing
back in check when it became all wonky and racing. The chains
on our porch swing weren't moving nearly as much as they used
to now that so many of our community members had moved on.
And the last teenager still coming around to borrow our lawn
mower would only get to see Luke's face since I had now taken to
hiding from door-knocks, kicked in the back of the knees when
the sun would go down on any given day.

There was no adventure to go on except survival; nobody to
save except for hopefully enough of myself that our boy wouldn't
have to grow up with a fraction of who his mother had hoped she'd
once been; no faith to have except mystery and daily bread; no
hard and fast lines, only weeping over the wreckage.

One afternoon, as we sat out on our back deck with a couple
shallow glasses of honey whiskey, cursing mosquitos, and watching our son splash away in his water table, I told Luke that I felt as
if I had spent my whole faith life blowing glass into window panes
of worldviews. I'd constructed the frames and then pied-pipered
any persuadable person into getting behind them. I told him that I
had spent such long hours building so many structures, deflecting
from one to another when they would inevitably be found faulty,
that they eventually became the cracked walls of a self-made maze.
And in this maze, I'd redirect and redirect at every wrong turn in
hopes of breaking free to build again before the walls could col-
lapse and steal my life (that is, my purpose).

But then, this most recent time, they'd fallen before I was able to escape and restructure. And now I laid buried beneath shards, wondering if I'd ever get the energy to sift what parts had been me and what parts had been God. My husband grabbed my hand as we sipped our Jack, as an ambulance crescendoed down our street, as our boy smiled with a mouthful of sand. And another day ended with a tiresomely tangled heart-web.

My job was fine. Our home was decently filled with warmth and working things out twenty-four hours at a time. My soul felt packed with so much rich and growing devotion to my kid and my partner that I could hardly stand it. But I no longer had a notion about what plausible, practical faithfulness in the kingdom of Jesus here on earth could even look like. It all sounded mythical now. People would speak to me as if I'd moved on to the next thing—as I'd done so many times before, as people do. I'd smile and say, "Things are good," or "We're all just a little tired," depending on the company.

But what was honest was that I wasn't sure what mattered to God anymore. And that this was more than terrifying; it was very sad. And that I felt broken. And that the shattered glass of my fallen walls had engulfed me and made the moving uncomfortable if not impossible. And that I wept often for my spirit's slow death and my lack of new causes or new cults to revive it.

It was a confusingly, miserably mundane time. I would label it cyclical and complex grief as the months paced on with little change, and I'd coax myself into being more gentle with me. I would call it tension, a season of no answers just moments, and I'd try to convince myself to not rush out of the in-between because maybe the in-between was just life now. If it was just life, it was a still a decent one, right? If it was not radical, purposeful, invigorating, or quintessential for the faith, it was still *good*, yes? How could I say that it wasn't?

But then, something happened, unhurriedly, with time.

And one morning, about a year and half of "decent" later, I began to realize (through a series of small moments and interactions) that when all of my doors had been closed and no new ones had swung open wide, something had perhaps been given the chance to open up inside of me instead. I had possibly not died after all. Or I had died, but now I was waking up. Maybe I was waking up new.

An Inner Door

The half-sized buggy I'd pushed all over our local grocery store was brimming with a haul that put my stubbornness on blast. *You always, every week, need a bigger cart,* I felt the aisle-walkers thinking. I'd shop with my headphones in: a new method for governing my social anxiety.

The tabloids hollered on about someone having someone's baby, someone getting into shape, someone getting out. I was sipping a double shot, trying to function in our perpetually sleepless life. Ahead, an older, white man—the age that warrants assistance—watched as the younger, black cashier pulled his easy-open soup cans and frozen dinners across the scanner. His wife, feeble and fading, waited like a statue by his side.

At the end of his grocery load, the cashier asked for his eighty dollars, which he thought he'd handed straight into her palm, I guess. I watched—as watching had become so much of what I did now. She counted sixty dollars, three twenties one by one, back to him. Gently, she asked for more cash to cover his charge. But, disoriented and panicked, or maybe sexist, or possibly racist, or maybe short on money or memory, his voice swelled like a siren.

"She took my money! That girl stole my money! This cashier put my money in her pocket! I gave her eighty, and she's saying I gave sixty!"

His wife reached for his elbow, dropping her head and recoiling into an embarrassed cringe. He wailed on and on until the whole store had about-faced toward us. The cashier stood tall and unruffled.

"Sir, let me call my manager who can take you to watch the cameras," she said with a steady disposition. It was an episode of misfortune, an outburst of several sad stories colliding: the accusation of the marginalized, the fear of the aging, the spouse who so loves her delusional partner. And there I was, unable to look away and so very tired. There I was, now unable to not feel all of their different lives and struggles inside of my bones.

Another cashier ran a card through the register one aisle over and pulled my piled-high cart into action again. I passed the strong, stoic woman being reamed, and I mouthed, "I'm so sorry . . ." The slow, mild shake of her head and half-roll of her eyes let me know that she was not surprised.

I pushed my bags into the back hatch of my car and scrambled into the driver's seat as quickly as possible. And then I sat there crying for all three of them and for me: for a world where my buggy could be so full when others were hungry and my soul so in need when others' were full; for a world where a young, black woman had had to learn how to stand so still and where growing older and growing disoriented could be so scary. I cried so hard that I felt my tears turn from pain to something that resembled, I don't know, maybe beauty?

In those long frozen-corn-thawing minutes in my car, brokenness began to feel like something I could no longer merely skirt like the Levite or fix like the Samaritan; but rather it was something to stare at, to study, to honor, to share. It was as if, in that Kroger parking lot, I could now see people at a lower layer of what made them up; like I was awake; like I could understand need because I had experienced it; like I could understand mercy because I had required it.

I began to wonder if mercy was an inner door opening that might allow me to pay better attention, to actually *see* the other humans on my road. I wondered if mercy was what could fill a person so full that judgement had little room left to breathe. I could not hate the older man in his belligerence, because I could see the parts of his hurt and history that looked like mine or like those whom I loved. I could not swoop in and save the cashier from her moment (outside of sharing what I'd seen and acknowledging my sorrow), because the moment was complex and she was strong, and because I felt like I truly needed someone to come in and save me. I could not reprimand the trembling wife with rage for a history of enabling indigence, because I no more knew their layers than they knew mine.

At this point, I felt that all I could do was listen, bear witness, say I'm sorry, feel their humanity, watch how their wounds could collide, weep in my car, and feel connected. It was more than my years of giving out of surplus; it was more than generosity, purpose, charity, answers, ideas. It was the first instance that I can remember being acutely aware of how my need (that cried out for relief, guidance, help, and grace day in and day out) could in fact be a road to another's soul. My eyes could see things now. And I could feel a faint pulse again.

The Best Conversation

Every Thursday, I began to clamber down the stairs of the Methodist Church in our neighborhood where I'd come on as the community arts director. Once a week, for an hour, I began volunteering to work the computer in the food pantry because I thought that this might be a way to continue to see my neighbors without blurring all of those still-tender emotional boundaries again.

As clients arrived, they were directed to one of two stations to be cleared for monthly groceries. One afternoon, a woman walked in, red folder in hand like someone unfamiliar with the run-around of assistance. Sitting down, frazzled and rushed, she asked what I would need from her while thumbing through files.

"What's the last four of your Social?" I started, trying to be casual, and comforting, and not overly either; trying to muster up any sort of energy that the extrovert in me had stolen when she skulked off of the OR table after the c-section two years before. "Let's see if you're in our system," I trailed off, hating how the word *system* tasted in my mouth, remembering Reagan, and remembering how low on funds we ourselves had been so recently. I felt like her peer, like her sister, and yet here I was again on the giving side of the desk.

"I'm not," she assured. "I'm new here, and new to this. I'm a country girl not quite cut out for the city."

"Oh, I'm a country girl too!" I widened my eyes. "Can't quite leave your car doors unlocked around here, huh?"

We small-talked about her kids and the hurdles she'd jumped to get them into three different schools. She mentioned, more than once, how she never thought she'd be in line for basics like food.

"Maybe I won't be next month," she crossed her fingers.

"You've got this," I said, ringing an invisible victory bell in the air and pausing to feel in my chest what it might be like to be her.

However, the niceties ceased when we both realized she was missing her budget sheet. That darn budget sheet that people had to receive by mail or retrieve in person at the state office was, at best, an afternoon's walk away. The pantry would be closed by the time she returned.

"I have a digital copy that I can . . ."

"I'm sorry ma'am, the rules are the rules," someone more seasoned than I inserted.

"Yeah, ok, I hear you," she mumbled, stuffing her papers into a folder and into a bag for a walk that would add hours to the now overwhelming task of getting two brown bags of food home to her kids. I waited for the booth to clear before reaching across the desk.

"I'm so sorry," I mouthed, thinking about the expenditures that exceeded our income all those months, thinking about what it was like to worry over whether or not I'd be able to feed my child, unable now to function in a delusion that I could be immune to her situation, aware of how we are only ever one misfortune or transition or death or ending away from standing in line for food ourselves, conscious of her need and now also of mine and how linked they were.

She cocked her head and stared at me, squinting. "That moment right there that you and I just had," she said slowly, "was the best conversation I have had all week."

"Me too," I said, telling the truth. "I really, really needed it."

In the coming months, mercy became the instances where someone would give themselves to me, not despite their hardship but precisely because of it. It became my growing ability to give myself to another—to my son, to a friend, to a stranger in the store—though I felt dried up and incompetent as well. Mercy was becoming that web of offering where people who knew that they needed each other constantly emptied out their almost-dry cups to fill another's—like how brown and black neighbors under the poverty line, mama circles, folks in recovery, and cancer patients take care of their own. Mercy was becoming the richest trade among the poorest folks.

Mercy was beginning to usher out the judgment that separated me from priest, or Levite, or Samaritan, or robber. It was inviting into my soul a sense of grace and wonder toward all sorts of differences, all sorts of poverties, all sorts of travelers along all sorts of paths. It was causing me to think differently and feel more deeply about the Syrian mother and all she'd lost and all she feared. It was causing me to think differently and feel more deeply about rich and poor, family and enemies, single parents, storm survivors, conservative preachers and the left-wing Jesus activists. It was making it harder to write off complexly beautiful and wounded people, to decide who they were and who they should be in a moment's time. I listened to stories about loneliness differently. I watched commercials that included even the slightest bit of humanity and would weep ugly, unbridled tears.

I began to feel it and them and this search for a meaningful life lower in my tissue than I ever had before labor, before loss; than I had before the last glass pane was obliterated and the last door shut; than I had before I understood my own limitations and therefore my own connection to others who were also limited and in need of God and God's people. The new—what felt like—cracking open and expansion of my heart was offering a fresh gentleness and revived tenderness for the people of the world who are all made in the image of God. All of them.

Mercy—and the motherhood, and the endings, and the questions and, God, the pain that brought me into mercy—was beginning to free me to feel on an untapped level of myself that left very little room for the fear and rigidity to which I was once saddled when I'd first asked Jesus to show me how and where to walk.

Mercy, I was learning, was the exchange of people who knew they needed each other. And I was finally one of them.

I am fighting tears as I type this because . . . I don't know why, for sure. Because it was one of the most humbling seasons of my life thus far? Because I felt more connected to the swollen, unrefined, and deep reality of what it means to be a person than ever before? Because it brought new definition to a word *(mercy)* that therefore brought new meaning to my faith that therefore indicated that I was still alive (or alive again) and not dead—and that this meant that God might still be doing something within me? Because it changed how I offered grace to people who do not live, or speak, or choose the same way that I do? Because it brought with it a faint whisper that maybe one day I could offer that same grace to my old self for having not loved like I had been so obviously and unshakeably loved?

"At the end of the day, Britney," an old college friend said to me around this time, "I still want answers. The sky is blue, and I don't know what to do when people tell me otherwise. There are universal truths to arrive at and ways for us to be walking. I just want to know them." I listened, trying to hear the layers. His sentiment sounded so very familiar. *Tell me the way, Jesus. The only way.*

But mercy was teaching me that to acknowledge that the sky was blue somewhere in the world did not mean that it was not also orange and gray elsewhere. And on the other side of the earth, it was likely pitch black and speckled with lights. Someone, somewhere was experiencing it as nonexistent: too many rainy days to even believe that there were any blue skies still to be enjoyed in this life. Someone in a plane above those dreary clouds could claim otherwise, having been exposed to the side of the sky where the sun still shines.

Someone hexed by the kaleidoscope of the Northern Lights, or blocked by buildings in New York City, or caught inside of a hurricane, could use other very fair descriptions. Outside of our atmosphere, one might look back on our vibrant planet, only to find that blue skies were not even a thing to be noticed anymore, much less argued over. More complex still were the ideas that people had once defined what it meant for something to be both "blue" and "sky"—that we had simply adopted such definitions.

This didn't have to mean that what we knew and could see (or even how we describe it) was not legitimate or real; but mercy was showing me that it probably meant that there was always more happening for more people than what we were experiencing ourselves. And my blue skies and New Zealand's black skies didn't have to contradict each other. It didn't have to mean that what I knew of what was above was wrong or to be tossed out. It just meant that the sky was bigger than blue. Maybe so, too, with God and faithfulness.

Mercy was teaching me about the preciousness of humanity and the human perspective. And I repented for having not embraced it before.

You Were Like an Angel

I returned to writing in these new and hard-to-define times. Writing, while it had long since been the thing that I could never not do, had now become the only way I knew how to process the layers of the world that I was now experiencing. It was becoming an agent of reconciliation for me to me—as is the mystery of art.

One week, as I wrote, I built up the nerve to reach out to John (my former D.C. friend and coworker) for the first time in eight years: twelve years since we'd parted ways in Philadelphia, eight years since I'd responded to his coming-out email with who knows what Levitical language. I wondered if his road had led him to a place where I could no longer be viewed as anything other than just another person in his timeline who had tried to make him something that he wasn't.

I wondered—as I sat in the cheap, teal lawn chairs beside our backyard fire pit, noting every character along that road to Jericho that I had been—if he had remembered me like I remembered me:

scared of being wrong, scared of letting others be wrong, under-exposed to difference, consumed with having answers, fluffy in Christian-speak, thrashing about Washington in my unexpected and unwelcome conversion.

"Hey my friend," my message began, "as I write about the last several years, the more recent experiences are easier to remember. But I'm having some difficulty tapping into my earlier twenties." I wanted to know if he would be willing to think back and share any descriptions about what my faith and outlook may have looked like or functioned as when we were in D.C.

"YES YES YES, oh you are seared into my life," a quick response followed along with a copy of the email I had sent to him eight years prior—the reply that I had long deleted out of fear of having done it poorly and having wounded him.

"Which is easier for you," I winced as I typed, "video call or written?" *Please say written.*

"I think this might be a better conversation to have where we can see each other," he answered.

I grew immediately worried about the reckoning I had welcomed. Here we would be, scouring through my past self, my previous characters, with a finetooth comb and the feelings of someone I had surely hurt. Here we would be, digitally face to face, voice to voice. Here we would be, in the judgment day for the one who got it wrong before she knew what mercy was, before she knew that she so needed it.

Let me have it, please don't hold back. I don't deserve it, I thought silently, wincing as his illuminated face popped up on my screen.

"I'll give you a couple of memories that stick out," John began after we'd put our headphones on and fought for a decent internet connection. He seemed how I last remembered him: bright, warm, enthusiastic.

He shared story after story that I never remembered happening. John talked about my ability to rein in the nonsense of our team and maintain what he remembers as a solid presence. I reminded him of our laundry trips and how the band of the summer had been the Killers. We wondered aloud where all the people we had met had ended up and shared parts of our time there that we had experienced privately and kept silent. I braced for the blow of the accusation. With each story that passed, I listened and interjected with nervous chuckles.

"You had a true sense of innocent conviction that maybe you think, when you're reflecting, 'Well that was just an ignorant girl from Louisiana.' But I'm expressing to you that maybe you haven't lost that—that conviction. It was always an incredibly beautiful thing."

In the recording of our conversation, you can hear a pause flecked with a periodic soft and confused "yeah, yeah" coming from my side of the line. And while waiting on the lashing that never came—while waiting on labels like oppressor or legalist, priest or Levite—his words pierced me: "Britney," he beamed, "you were like an angel pulling me out."

More than forgiven, I felt pardoned. More than seen, I felt loved.

"When you responded to my Facebook message, asking to speak face to face," I finally said, pushing back different kinds of tears than I had prepared for, "I immediately became so nauseated thinking about what I must have said to you in that email, how I must have injured you as the person I was during our time together. I felt as if you were going to show me a picture of myself at thirteen with braces, and bad hair, and all that I didn't yet know. But the way that you remember our summer is a version of me that I think is far more graceful than I am able to recall."

With a warm smile that told me we still belonged to each other, he said, "Totally. Maya Angelou says we remember how people make us feel, not how they were or what they said. Be gentle with you. That's the same advice I give to me."

Feeling blindsided by the gift of John's big mercy, I replied, "There was a moment in the last few years where it changed in my head that we don't have to have all the answers but we have to be space-makers for people to be all of themselves in our company. What's been hard for me is reflecting now on all the times that I refused the company of someone, or an important piece of someone, because of who I was at the time along my road."

"But Britney, we've all done that," he sounded so gentle and motherly. "Showing mercy to yourself, forgiving yourself, I think it's the hardest part of our journey for the rest of our lives. We have to hold who we were, and we have to also forgive them."

With the digital box of John's face closing out of sight once we'd said our goodbyes, I realized that loving one's neighbor as one loves themselves had become suddenly so much less about prioritizing others through selfless acts above selfish ambition. But rather, it was now about being able to better embrace the humanity and the varying journey of another because one was able to embrace who they themselves are, who they've been, and who they'll be; to hold those parts of their path and to also forgive them; to do more than forgive them, but to love them.

I felt, in this unexpectedly divine moment, able to now love in a new way because John had so clearly and unreservedly loved me.

John had loved me like Jesus loves me.

I could now maybe love similarly, because I had first been loved at various versions of me.

I could better love me and those who did and did not look like, act like, think like, serve like, speak like, choose like, journey like me. Everyone who had ever been the *other* in my life was now, on good days, just another God-made person who deserved my consideration and not just my correction, who deserved to be treated as if I had birthed them right on out of my body—that kind of connection. Everyone, including old me, was becoming someone new—or could.

John was the Samaritan to my wounded, roadside self when just ten years before I'd only been able to imagine the scenario in reverse. He crouched beside my broken body and showed me how a neighbor loves, and then showed me how I could love me (and others) in the very same way.

John taught me that self-love was not the default that I'd always assumed it was when the seeker first bantered with Jesus about the biggest, best, and fullest life. We could not truly love our needy neighbor as ourselves until we loved ourselves for who we truly were and had been. We could not love ourselves until we knew ourselves as needing the mercy we were hoping to give.

I could not know resurrection, I could not sincerely *go and do likewise,* until I'd been the one dying on the ground and desperate for another's merciful love; until I could see my life in the lives of all the other travelers and say, "I forgive us, too."

"You were like an angel pulling me out," said the angel who was pulling me out.

I felt myself get up off of the ground: like second life, like born again, like Easter. I felt compelled to take those colorful, shattered shards and begin making art out of their chaos, binding together shapes that mattered: the good, the gross, the guided by God. I felt intricate and storied, like stained glass in old chapels—more storied than solid panes built like idols for my ego's control. I felt storied like a multitude of characters on the road to Jericho whom love had so generously washed over.

I was now a piece of something made of pieces, something that pain had broken and mercy had saved so that I might learn to *really* be a neighbor to me; so that I might learn to really be a neighbor to another.

10

Likewise

The Listener

The story is read again, but now it all sounds different as you listen:

"What's most important?" the seeker's voice cracks. He's desperate, you remember.

"What do you already know?" Jesus reminds.

"What God has told us." His face blotches with nerves. Oh, how he hates that it does that.

"That's right," Jesus nods. Thank God, the seeker inhales.

"But wait! But wait. Wait, please, can you clarify? Be specific? Spell it out exactly how we are to do what we are to do?"

As the seeker calls out, clawing onto the passing moment, your mother-heart aches to hold him—to hold the him who looks like you. He is so worried to get wrong what is right in front of him; so scared to miss what is already his, what was already yours all along.

Jesus's response, a story about who does and doesn't stop, feels like a new narrative now. It is simpler and more complex. It is a part of who you've been and who you're becoming. It is a part of who the seeker is becoming, though he doesn't yet know it. It is layered, and you wonder what levels you've yet to discover. It makes you feel no longer anxious to be the one who got it right, but rather, you are loved and grateful and that is enough.

Grateful to have been on the road.

To still be on the road.

To be both a recipient and agent of the mercy of God that binds us all in the richest exchange of need, forgiveness, and hopeful connection that will make for another world.

Love Never Fails

As we walk down the front steps of the home in which we still live, I glance over at the hollowed community-house across the street from ours that reminds me daily that what we build and believe in is often subject to change. And though I still wonder how long I will grieve the finite reality of experiences so special, I am grateful for what is constant and also for what has changed.

As Luke and our son head toward the sidewalk, I recall the words that were once cut out of pale orange, polka dot, sage floral, and maroon plaid scrapbook paper for our community's dining space. The letters that spelled out "Love Never Fails" were ducttaped to the wall in the very beginning and lasted until the very end. For years, an ever rotating door of people would pass by and press the drooping "s" back into place, and we'd joke about the symbolism of its relentless falling. Close life with people had been a continuous reminder that love did not, would not, could not leave, and that we never get to stop working to push it back up despite the evolution of ourselves.

Silently making our way to the bayou where we walk for serotonin in the evenings, a slideshow from the last two decades flashes through my head, set to the sound of a song about gratitude. And for the first time in my life, I am not cringing while looking backward, and I am not running to move forward.

Our son gallops in front of us with two dead leaves each the size of his beautiful round head in hand. He calls every bird a duck while inviting them into his long, comfy arms. The dirt down by the bayou is dark and wet—gritty like brownie batter. The three of us are crushing clover underneath while water collects down the drainage walls, creating silver dimples as it carries all the ducks and non-duck ducks to different parts of the city.

My kid's indigo and lime-yellow hoodie pulled up over the back of his feathery hair makes me wonder, in a refreshing thought, how the big and now bigger God may be looking at me in this moment: all of me, and all of who I've been, and all of who I may grow into as I wait and listen and walk. Maybe God looks on me with this same, impossibly deep maternal love that courses through my veins now as I embrace and am embraced by mercy—the mercy that found me when I'd lost me, when I'd lost all I'd fashioned to hold and inform me.

As we stroll behind little legs in this new season of our thirties, of job-change, of turning over rocks to find interests and community, I still fight the addiction to right answers and big purpose every day. It feels like I am in recovery. I find myself waiting for direction from God as if it is a baton that I am poised to dash off with once it arrives. I look for it, mostly subconsciously, in the form of titles, or radical lifestyles, or movements, or a group so alive and stimulating that one can't help but to join them.

But also, I'm here—sixteen years since becoming the priest, thirteen since the Levite, eleven since the Samaritan, nine since the innkeeper, six since the robber, and three since the wounded and the saved—finding that the great discipline of my life in these days is to allow this merciful love to be enough; to dedicate myself to finding it in the corners and cracks of this world; to yield to its deep and mysterious waters that help me love all parties who are entangled in the injustices I am aching to change; to heal the earth by first going inward when I've only ever so desperately known how to go outward; and to trust the journey.

Recovery looks like small things right now: less envisioning giant gardens and more planting of microscopic seeds; less building massive window panes and more beauty out of their pieces; less megaphone-led movements and more minutes spent witnessing the movement that is taking place within my very soul and in the souls of those around me; less conclusions and more processes.

It sometimes looks like investing a bit in our neighborhood's local school or planting hydrangeas that symbolize some form of commitment-to-place in our front yard. It looks like dabbling in New Monasticism (again) by reading Erin Wasinger and Sarah Arthur's book called *The Year of Small Things: Radical Faith for the Rest of Us,* which dropped into my lap at such a merciful time. It looks like making murals with our neighbors through my job, which is a part of the church that we recently joined. It looks like leaving work at work, which is a new and odd phenomenon for someone who has always equated employment with calling and calling as needing to be emotionally tumultuous to be of God. It looks like staring longer at the suffering of the world and embracing the pain that this suffering is supposed to make me feel. It looks like meditating on the names of the oppressed and oppressors as the children of God that they are. It looks like third ways, and sharing food, and trying to hear. It looks like liturgy, and opening our front door, and being close to the poor, and committing to healthy conflict and to generosity and to prayer.

And on good recovery days, it looks like mercy.

I see mercy in those who are willing to be the midwives of another's spirit instead of the shamers of what is not yet born. I see mercy in people who, instead of lashing out at groups whose ideologies feel offensive and threatening, choose to be honest about the world they see while committing to rephrasing through paint and poetry and personal stories until we can hear each other. I see mercy in those who know that if we want something different, we have to do something different, like find and craft the parables and learn ourselves as multiple characters within them.

I see mercy as being greater than judgement in those who are able and willing to step outside of their own limited perspectives and consider another's—who are not so willing to die on hills of blue-only skies but who are getting close to people in order to better understand vast perspectives. I see mercy as what could move the church and our country forward as we seek to see and learn (and love) ourselves as we've truly been, asking for and offering forgiveness that we may connect and heal in our becoming. I see mercy most vibrantly in the people who know that the road to Jericho must be redeemed because the trauma caused on its shoulders is not of God, but who can work towards that end with deep and lavish compassion for each and every character who walks it because they have known themselves as all of them. I see mercy in those who know that demonizing is dehumanizing, and dehumanizing is not an option for we who are grateful to have been offered an outstretched hand.

But mercy-seeing is constant work in this world—in my world. Something will happen today, and my ability to recognize myself in someone who has hurt me (or someone I love, or someone who is vulnerable or marginalized) will fly right on out the door. My anger and my damn mouth will take over, and it will be as if I was never the wounded who needed passersby to kneel in the story at all. But tonight, when I lay my head down on my pillow, I will think of my road and all those I have been. I'll think of all those who have loved me despite the roles that I have played. I'll think of how we're bound, and I'll hold that person in my heart as if I labored them right out of myself. If it's a good day, I'll forgive me; and then I'll pray to be able to see our intertwined and mirrored existences quicker if not first the next time.

And so this is my hope for the world (and this book that has surfaced on a road riddled with more faith deconstructions and reconstructions than I ever imagined would be mine): that we will receive each other with tenderness, connection, and mercy quicker if not first the more we walk; that we will trust that no one is limited to how we experience them in a moment, not even in a season, not even ourselves; that we will encounter mercy and that we will let that mercy well up inside of us, drawing us back from our debates and our slander, helping us tap into the Holy Spirit who gives us creativity to reframe injustices with beauty until they feel personal so that we can *actually* make headway in our healing; that we will not stop reading Scriptures or building water wells or growing community or fighting injustices, but that we will do all of this and so much *more* with a tender and broken heart for every life that is involved; that mercy will be the inner door through which we see how much damage our religious answer-pushing and way-demanding has caused; that the sensitivity that mercy brings may then create honest-to-God pathways to another, that we can be made new together.

And I hope you will forgive you for the you that you have been.

I hope you'll forgive me for the same.

And I hope that this can mean that we might remember how we're intertwined in the merciful love of God that never, ever, ever leaves us unchanged and uncared for on this path, be us robber or radical, Samaritan or saint.

Maybe the way is in the walking. Maybe it has been all along.

Maybe the road has always been about mercy.

Maybe mercy is unfolding.

Maybe mercy is loving one's enemy like you need them.

Maybe mercy is giving out of one's need and not out of one's surplus.

Maybe mercy is not jailing someone into how you first experience them.

Maybe mercy is knowing that we are all becoming new; or we all have the ability to become new.

Maybe mercy is accountability drenched in self-awareness and tenderness.

Maybe mercy is exponentially greater than judgement.

Maybe mercy surfaces at the death bed of our control.

Maybe mercy is what provokes truly God-inspired service.

Maybe mercy is gentle midwifery for the spirit.

Maybe mercy is a mirror.

Maybe mercy is a leveler.

Maybe mercy is a binder for mutual liberation.

Maybe mercy is the toe in the door for unconditional love.

Maybe mercy is first forgiveness.

Maybe mercy is the story of how we are compelled to kneel down because someone first knelt down for every version of us that we have ever been.

Maybe mercy is taking the name of our other and putting it in the sentence: "_____ is a child of God."

Maybe mercy is holding the pain that this sentence conjures and letting it teach us.

Maybe mercy is meditating on how our faith has manifested in our world. Maybe mercy is not throwing the baby out with its bathwater, but instead is about the contemplative life that helps us discern what practices to keep and which to not.

Maybe mercy is a constant deconstruction to remind us how big is our Creator.

Maybe mercy is a good bit mystery.

Maybe mercy is complicated. And simple.

Maybe mercy gives us less fear and more light.

Maybe mercy gives us more stories and fewer answers.

Maybe mercy is what informs the work that we do to truly make another world because what ignites our fire for change is our gratitude and self/other love and not our hate.

Maybe mercy is what makes us neighbor, after all . . .

We make the turn around the bayou to head back to our house just as Bridger empties his pockets full of pretzels for all of God's feathered creatures to enjoy. The soil underneath me today smells of home—all the homes I have ever had that smelled like soil. I am thankful for having grown, and to be growing still, on a road edged with the soil of home and soaked with misadventures so wild that

I might be led to the deep and deeply complex mercy of God and (would you believe it?) for today, peace. For today, there's peace and hope (again) in the good news that God loves the world, and God's love is in the world, and it's invited us into its depths in order to make the world better. And that I get to keep figuring out what that means alongside other sacredly pieced-together people.

"Love Never Fails," the letters said, always—maybe the only steady presence in all those changing slides. I suppose it didn't. And I suppose it hasn't still.

Bibliography

Alcorn, Randy. *The Grace and Truth Paradox: Responding with Christlike Balance.* Colorado Springs, CO: Multnomah, 2003.

Arthur, S., and E. Wasinger. *The Year of Small Things: Radical Faith for the Rest of Us.* Grand Rapids, MI: Brazos, 2017.

Claiborne, S., J. W. Hartgrove, and E. Okoro. *Common Prayer: A Liturgy for Ordinary Radicals.* Grand Rapids, MI: Zondervan, 2010.

Claiborne, Shane. *The Irresistible Revolution: Living as an Ordinary Radical.* Grand Rapids, MI: Zondervan, 2006.

Manning, Brennan. *The Ragamuffin Gospel: Good News for the Bedraggled, Beat-Up, and Burnt-Out.* Colorado Springs, CO: Multnomah, 2005.

Schwartz, Timothy T. *Travesty in Haiti: A True Account of Christian Missions, Orphanages, Food Aid, Fraud and Drug Trafficking.* N.p.: Timothy Schwartz, 2008.